HEARTS, MINDS

HEARTS, MINDS & INTERESTS

Britain's Place in the World

PETER UNWIN

Peter Un—

P

PROFILE BOOKS

Blakeney

Oct '04

First published in Great Britain in 1998 by
Profile Books Ltd
62 Queen Anne Street
London W1M 9LA

in association with
David Davies Memorial Institute of International Studies
2 Chadwick Street
London SW1P 2EP

Printed in Great Britain by Biddles Ltd

A CIP catalogue record for this book is available from the British Library.

ISBN 1 86197 078 1

For Julia; and in memory of my father

Contents

Preface

For most of my lifetime Britain has been adrift in the world, unsure where it belongs. To Winston Churchill the 1930s were the locust years, consumed by appeasement and unpreparedness. In the war the British found a worthy role for themselves in the fight against Hitler. But the war brought also a suspicion of decline, a suspicion which in the early postwar years hardened into a conviction which haunted British thinking for half a century.

Over the years many observers have documented that decline; some have challenged it; and others have tried to set against it the evidence of success.[1] The judgment between these views has become a major issue in politics, and the thesis of national decline has provided a natural theme for electoral manifestos and knockabout debate. The issue has preoccupied the media and the political and chattering classes, and two generations have imbibed something of this concern with their mother's milk. To change the national mood has been a task with which statesmen have wrestled, more often than not unsuccessfully. If Britain today is more cheerful about itself than it has been in recent decades, there is no certainty that it will stay that way.

This thesis of failure and decline is based more on domestic than on international performance. But when comparison is not between present and past, it is between home and abroad. The most impressive documentation of Britain's decline was found in comparison with other countries: an all-powerful, innovative United States; a Germany and Japan recovering from defeat and going on to surpass Britain economically; a self-confident France and an Italy proclaiming its *sorpasso*;

and eager Asian tigers which seemed likely to continue to take markets from us well into the next century. So domestic unease fed on international comparison, and the British convinced themselves that they were less effective than other people.

There was also a purely international character to these concerns which extended beyond comparisons. Churchill's locust years were consumed by the fear of Hitler and of war. When war came, it brought with it the chance to recover our self-confidence as one of the Second World War's Big Three. But international evidence of our weakness came close on the heels of the end of the fighting, with our forced departures from Greece and Palestine. Indian independence in 1947 started a process which ran, almost uninterrupted, through our imperial history to the return of Hong Kong to China 50 years later. And each independence ceremony in turn provided a moving, sometimes agonising, reminder of a diminished status in the world.

∽

Snaps from my autobiographical photograph album illustrate the stages in the process, and its emotional as much as its intellectual consequences. I can just remember my father explaining that the Hiroshima bomb had moved the United States into a league quite removed from lesser powers such as Britain. I was 16 when the United States Air Force launched its Flying Fortress fleet on a great demonstration of strength and reassurance up and down Britain at the time of the Berlin Blockade. I reported for duty in the Foreign Office for the first time on the day the Suez Canal was nationalised, and three months later began to understand the damage Anthony Eden's adventure had done to Britain's international reputation. A few years later, in Japan, I was charged with organising some minor Commonwealth get-together at the margins of an international conference, and it took a kindly New Zealander to explain that it might be better not to call it the "British Commonwealth" on the invitations. Our travails over European Community membership consumed much of my early middle age. I have seen what I thought I would never see, the collapse of the Soviet Union and of the Soviet Empire. And throughout my career I have heard, like all my colleagues, the constant pitter-pat of questions about the utility to a diminished Britain of the diplomatic activities by which we earned our daily bread.

In 1979 the Foreign and Commonwealth Office sent me on a sabbatical year to Harvard, where I turned my mind to the questions that had lain behind most of my work in the previous 20 years. Where did Britain belong in the world, where did it want to be, where did its interests take it, what were the strengths and weaknesses, opportunities and threats which shaped its choices? My thoughts became a paper on British foreign policy in the 1980s, which came to the unremarkable conclusion that Britain's place was in Europe; that Europe must be seen as complementary with rather than antithetical to the Atlantic and the United States; and that it was in our interests to ensure that Europe kept itself open to the outside world. More originally, I argued for economic and monetary union as a centrepiece in the development of that European Community: a reasonable argument, I thought, even if I advanced it ten years too soon.[2]

But in 1979 I misread the prospects for the 1980s. They turned out to be the years in which the assumptions of the postwar decades were stood on their head. In 1982 Britain threw calculation out of the window and set off on an emotional crusade to rescue the Falkland Islands from Argentinian occupation. It succeeded triumphantly, if by the narrowest of margins, and for a time Britain convinced itself and others that it had recovered its self-confidence along with the islands. Domestic circumstance helped too: Margaret Thatcher's revolution imposed strains, unprecedented since the 1930s, on Britain's social cohesion, but checked the country's economic decline and seemed to promise a strong competitive base for a new assertiveness in international affairs. At the end of the 1980s came freedom for the Soviet Union's East European empire, the collapse of Communism and of the Soviet Union itself, and the end of the cold war which had for so long shaped most thinking about the world. And in 1997 a new government claimed to offer a new Britain a new start.

Britain is only now beginning to get to grips with the very different world that emerged from the year of miracles, 1989, and the years of astonishing change which have followed it. Too much of our attention has been taken up with strife over Europe: within the European Community, over the exact nature, scope and extent of the European

Union, and at home, over our relationship with it and with the rest of the European continent. At the same time Russia has gone into a decline from which it will take decades to recover and the United States has assumed even greater salience as the only remaining global power. The Japanese miracle has paled and the east Asian tigers, still promising so much, are looking distinctly mangy. China, with Hong Kong recovered, is approaching the status of a global power. In Africa, the former Yugoslavia and some of the old Soviet Union's republics, the world has been confronted with the sort of regional and national crises that the rigid order of the cold war seemed to have abolished. Economic, industrial and technological forces have begun to make our planet a single global entity. So Britain, like all its neighbours, is faced with a vastly changed world as it tries to define where it belongs in it

$\backsim$

In the spring of 1995 a traditionally cautious Foreign and Commonwealth Office gathered up its skirts and stepped out on to a public stage. It had for some time been cautiously opening its councils to outsiders, with staff exchanges, seminars with academics and the publication of annual reports of its doings. Now it went further, going into partnership with the Royal Institute of International Affairs to mount a major conference on Britain and the world. The press characterised it as an attempt to distract attention from the Conservative government's difficulties with its European policy or as the swan song of a Foreign and Commonwealth Secretary who was leaving government for the City. To those who attended, it seemed rather an attempt to engage an unusually broad range of opinion-formers in discussion of this new world; of Britain's options and interests in it; and of the ever growing interpenetration of the domestic and international factors which policy has to take into account.

The conference was only a qualified success. Too many bits of government took up too much of the time available for exposition; and in the time available for discussion too many vested interests insisted on having their self-interested say. All the same, it was a noteworthy occasion: if it was not well done, it was nevertheless surprising, and encouraging, that it should be done at all. The David Davies Memorial

Institute of International Studies, of which I had just become director, felt that it too should contribute to the process of debating Britain's place in the world, and produced a pamphlet for distribution to the conference participants.[3]

The institute was encouraged by the responses to this 12-page paper to take discussion of the subject further, and established a study group to examine it. It brought together individuals from different disciplines, backgrounds and age groups for a series of informal discussions. Out of those discussions came the decision to produce this book. Every member of the group contributed both to general discussion and to the written development of the argument. None of them is responsible for the final product, and none of them would be prepared to endorse every part of it. But there would have been no book without their contributions, and I am grateful to each of them for their help in writing it.[4]

The group set itself to examine Britain's place in today's world, and its prospects over the next 20 years. I hope the result is intellectually respectable, but it is not a work of scholarship. Nor is it an exhaustive examination of the myriad issues which have to be addressed by any major country in the conduct of its foreign policy. The aim was to bring together the factors which condition British attitudes to the outside world and to analyse Britons' feelings about the United States, about Europe and the European Union, the east Asian countries and the uneasily stirring Islamic giant, and about the developing world, so much of which was shaped by British imperial rule. To put beside this examination we tried to summarise the power of all these places to help Britain or to harm it, and to see whether conventional assessments of opportunity and threat match British instincts. We were as interested in emotions as in facts, in hearts as much as minds.

We wanted to look also at Britain's relationships with the systems and structures that try to hold the world together in peaceful and profitable coexistence. They are regional, like the European Union; or global, like the United Nations. They can be essentially governmental: integrationist, like the European Union, or loosely cooperative, like the United Nations. They are sharply focused, like NATO, or general, almost familial, like the Commonwealth. The non-governmental organisations provide a different kind of structure. So do the transnational corporations, which the man in the street scarcely recognises as politically significant but which in quiet fact rival the clout of governments. Information plays as big a part as organisations in binding our world together, whether it be conventionally transmitted, like the BBC's "nation speaking peace unto nation", or the technical, financial, computerised, cybernetic information flows that have given us, almost without our noticing it, a globally wired world.

All these things affect countries' domestic as well as international concerns. This is one reason why people have such difficulty coming to terms with the ambitions and requirements of the European Union: a remote matter one moment, presuming to dictate the content of our sausages the next. Some think of Toyota as a powerful element of Japan Inc and a worldwide investor; to others it merely provides a tediously reliable motor car. An organisation like Friends of the Earth campaigns globally in one mode and solicits our pennies in another. It is this constant interaction of domestic and external in everyday affairs which takes this book beyond foreign policy as it is conventionally understood, and even beyond the broader swathes of national policy, into the instincts that shape our thoughts and the emotions that stir within our breasts.

꿈

In writing this book I have been driven by a conviction that in my lifetime Britain has done less well than it could, and than it must if it is to prosper in a scratchy and competitive world. But foreign observers remind us of our blessings. Read, for example, Raymond Seitz's impressions of his time as American ambassador at the Court of St James's[5] or consider Vitali Vitaliev's views as he compares our fortunate state with his ancestral Russia or adopted Australia.[6] Or look at the sentences with which Bill Bryson ended his account of an exploration of these small islands:

> "What an enigma Britain will seem to historians when they look back on the second half of the twentieth century. Here is a country that fought and won a noble war, dismantled a mighty empire in a generally benign and enlightened way, created a far-seeing welfare state – in short, did nearly everything right – and then spent the rest of the century looking on itself as a chronic failure. The fact is

that this is still the best place in the world for most things – to post a letter, go for a walk, watch television, venture out for a drink, go to a museum, use the bank, get lost, seek help, or stand on a hillside and take in a view."[7]

Perhaps few of us, Britons or outside observers, see Britain in exactly that light. By many another measure, it is a less satisfactory place than Bryson believes. But in his generosity of judgment, he reminds us of something we too easily forget. Uncertain of itself and of its international importance as Britain may be, it nevertheless brings a quality and distinction of its own to the world.

Peter Unwin
February 1998

1 Peter Clarke, *Hope and Glory, Britain 1900–1990* (London: Allen Lane, 1996).

2 Peter Unwin, "British Foreign Policy Opportunities", *International Affairs*, London, Spring and Summer 1981.

3 Peter Unwin, *Where Britain Belongs* (London: David Davies Memorial Institute, 1995).

4 The Study Group's members were Christopher Beauman, George Bull, Vincent Cable, Stephen Chan, Peter Gottwald, Matthew Kidd, Sally Morphet, Michael Palliser, Larry Siedentop, Mary Unwin and Richard Whitman. Martin Morland, who became involved at a later stage, contributed much to the work.

5 Raymond Seitz, *Over Here* (London: Weidenfeld & Nicolson, 1998).

6 Vitali Vitaliev, *Dreams on Hitler's Couch* (London: Richard Cohen Books, 1997).

7 Bill Bryson, *Notes From a Small Island* (London: Black Swan, 1996).

1   Is the state immortal ?

We live in a world of states, and our own is for most of us the focus of our loyalties. But other things compete for interest and commitment, and yet others perform some of the functions that used to fall unquestioned to the state. If the 19th century saw the state's development and the 20th its apotheosis, the 21st may be the century of its decline. This is a book about a state and its people, about Britain and the British and where in the world they belong. If the future of the state in general may be in question, so may the future of Britain as a state. We need therefore to look in the first instance at two general questions. Where does the state as an institution stand in 1998, and is it likely to endure in a form we would recognise in the first quarter of the next century?

In most developed countries the state does not enjoy today the almost automatic loyalty and commitment that our great-grandfathers gave it. Men no longer go unquestioningly to war or invest in their country a transcendent, almost mystic significance. Patriotism has its place and it is more assertive in some countries than others. But most people identify also with other levels of organisation: with local community or city, Scotland the fair or German *Land* or American state, with an ethnic group or a special interest group, with region or continent or indivisible humanity. As industrialised societies have become more sophisticated, individuals' investment in alternative, multiple, "porous" or "layered"[1] identities has strengthened, at the expense of dedication to the state.

Throughout most of the West, people are tired of politics and the pretensions of politicians. Since they claim to act and speak for us in the organisation, administration and representation of the state, disillusion with them has become disillusion with the state. Individuals seek instead outlets for their political passions in good causes or pressure groups. Some work happily enough in a national context, but others seek a wider stage, feeding the world's hungry or saving its whales, or a narrower one, preoccupied with local housing or the fate of suburban trees. Each further distracts attention from the state.

Thus there is a sense that there is something *passé* about the concept of the state as a unique focus of loyalty, and also about those who speak for it. As many of the state's traditional functions are usurped by others, scepticism about its pretensions grows. In western Europe and north America at least, it is under sustained questioning from the most talkative and influential among its citizens.

At the same time the old primacy of the state is under pressure from wider groupings, which have succeeded in eroding what was once its very particular and exclusive authority. Almost every country in the world has committed itself in the last half century to a vast range of international obligations through the United Nations and its agencies, through international economic institutions and under international law. Its members may affect to despise the United Nations and be reluctant to fund it, but they nevertheless send their troops to die in its blue helmets. Most of the Western world has placed its security in the hands of NATO. Fifteen western European countries have committed themselves to the uncertain destination of "ever closer union" set out in the Treaty of Rome in 1957, and have given the European Union the legally enforceable right to govern more aspects of our daily lives than the state itself presumed to regulate two generations ago. And in the World Trade Organisation, the IMF and the World Bank, states accept, in their differing degrees, the economic authority of global bodies that they do not directly control.[2]

It is states themselves that have given all these powers their importance, and in theory they can take back what they have bestowed. But they are locked in mutual dependencies that express themselves in these groupings. For most states, untrammelled freedom of action is unattainable, and even for the most powerful, the United States, its pursuit in every particular is not worth the candle. Theories of sovereignty aside, almost every country today shares much of its power and authority with international, functional and regional organisations.

↶

Yet the most pervasive challenge to the authority of the state does not come from the growth of new interests and loyalties within its borders, nor from the world's international and regional organisations. It comes instead from forces which take no patently political form but which bring about profoundly political effects.

Of these the most powerful is international business. Yesterday's businessmen asserted that their concern was not with politics but with market share and profit. To responsibility to shareholder and customer they have added in the last 30 years obligations to their "stakeholders" – to employees, the environment, the community, social betterment – while still insisting that business does not presume to usurp the authority and responsibility of government. Yet the operations of international business have a collective impact on politics, economics, international relations and society greater than that of most national governments.

Robert Reich, Secretary of Labor in the first Clinton administration, documented that impact.[3] He argued that international business operates globally, using systems that ignore frontiers. A major company is internationally competitive or it is marked for extinction. It deploys its productive capacity worldwide, overriding national frontiers as it does so; governments compete to attract its investment, for the sake of the production and employment it brings. It markets its goods around the world, and national predilections yield to a homogenised global taste. To finance their operations multinational companies use international exchanges, whose flows of billions of dollars dwarf the financial operations of governments. Their directors sometimes identify, Reich argued, less with their country than their company, and more with their international peers than their compatriots.

There is an element of exaggeration in Reich's argument, but he points down a path that international businessmen may increasingly follow. Thirty years ago Jean-Jacques Servan-Schreiber advanced a comparable proposition. He argued that American-based international business was successfully exploiting European markets as if they were one, and in the process overwhelming the national preoccupations of governments. It was American businessmen rather than the Europeans who were making a reality of Europe's pretensions to build a single market like the United States.[4] Since then, the phenomenon Servan-Schreiber discerned has become a global one; Asian and European companies have joined the Americans; and companies operating across borders have become so international that it is immaterial where their head offices are based. The process is driven by commercial considerations but it has a political effect. Beside the world's game played by statesmen, a rival game played by international business and banking has sprung up, and it has begun to marginalise the operations of all but the most substantial national governments.

Something similar is happening in the world of voluntary and not-for-profit organisations. Their activities may extend as far as those of business, if more tenuously. Peter Willetts has documented their contribution to the United Nations' agenda.[5] They help shape policy on the environment, gender, development and human rights. Their campaigns build support which is as much political as financial. Voluntary groups maintain that they are concerned with their good causes and not with politics or economics. But in pursuit of their aims they monitor, criticise, check and occasionally humiliate governments and international companies. They set themselves to fight for representative government, human rights or accountable administration in a way which gets them into the interstices of national life. They have a role in emergencies which cannot fail to take political expression. When states fail, Médicins sans Frontières and Oxfam stand beside United Nations agencies to bring relief.

There is also a technological, communications and cultural component of these international forces. The new technologies cannot be confined within physical frontiers. Eastern Europe's "velvet revolution" was sustained by the fax machine. The Internet serves the academic and the pornographer just as electronic money transfer serves the banker. The computer makes data processing on a global basis an everyday reality. Satellite communications can get a story out of the most remote corner of the earth just as television can spread it wherever there is electricity. The clockwork radio can take it even further into the desert or the bush. Although the BBC and CNN still wear a national stamp of origin on their sleeve, the communications revolution which they lead is a global phenomenon, which has built a global information base. All these things undermine the state just as surely as the power of international business or the influence of international non-governmental organisations.

Yet it is not an open-and-shut argument. In most of the developed world national governments still dispense getting on for half of their countries' wealth. The state remains the essential source of security for its citizens.[6] In many countries, central government has assumed new areas of responsibility at home as it surrenders responsibilities abroad.[7] Today it regulates educational, environmental, health and even ethical standards, for example, in a way that would have astonished our grand-parents. The state, like any other old-established organisation, has an eternally surprising capacity to reinvent itself. And our country retains for most of us the power to pluck at our heart strings.

So great powers like the United States, Japan and China will not be willing to abdicate their authority, either as national players in the world's game or as instruments of organisation with calls on their peoples' loyalties. Their governments retain a sublime confidence in their authority and legitimacy within their boundaries, and the United States tries to extend its reach outside them through extra-territorial legislation. The post-communist world is alive with na-tionalism, at best euphoric with the reassertion of long submerged identities, at worst instinct with xenophobia and fascism. Most of the countries of the developing world have enjoyed their independence for less than half a century: their leaders too are not going to sur-render it to wider brotherhoods.

Even the states of western Europe, which have gone furthest in pooling authority and identity, have not ceased to assert the one and re-joice in the other. The European Community's role in saving the na-tions from their own excesses has been as important as its creation of a new centre of transnational authority and identity.[8] As the role of Brus-sels has grown, the roles of Paris, Bonn and London have not been fa-tally diminished. For the moment the nations of western Europe are expressing themselves with renewed vigour and self-confidence.

⌒

The prospects for the state are threfore uncertain ones. Challenges to its primacy have multiplied in the last half century, yet it wields powerful resources of its own. It is quite as capable as its rivals of adaptation and re-invention. Confident forecasts that the state is on the road to obsolescence or extinction lack clearcut contemporary evidence. Douglas Hurd called it "both immortal and incompetent".[9] We need to dip further into the history of the territorial state and its competitors, to see whether the past can give us any guidance to the future.

You can trace manifestations of the state as far back as you like in history, but for the limited practical purposes of a book about Britain, the hunt for its origins starts in Europe in the sixteenth century. Renaissance monarchs in France, Spain and England then began the process of building European states, as far as possible identifiable with nations. Successive generations ever since have elaborated and extended the concept and practice of statehood.[10]

For getting on for 500 years before the Renaissance, the political and social organisation of Europe had been shaped by a variety of powers: by the pope and the emperor themselves, and by kings, abbots, bishops, burghers, magnates and lesser nobles under their overall authority. When 16th-century kings set about carving territorial order out of this complexity, they undermined the unity of Christendom quite as much as they destroyed centres of power inferior to their own. In the process they created distinctiveness in place of the old common identity; they linked their territorial ambitions with inchoate cravings for nationhood, grouping together people who usually spoke the same language, who identified themselves by their difference from those who did not, and who could be prevailed upon to march to the same drum. The Reformation swept away the universal papacy and set religion beside language and allegiance as a measure of distinction between states. In 1648 the Treaty of Westphalia gave international endorsement to the structures which individual kings had built, and the territorial state became the recognised unit within which other structures – economic, social and cultural – evolved. In 1776 the American Revolution brought democracy to the national brew and in 1789 La Grande Nation added its contribution of liberty, equality and fraternity.

Napoleon might have set Europe on another course, in which national states gave way to a continent-wide empire; but by 1813, at Leipzig, aptly named the Battle of the Nations, he was down and by 1815, at Waterloo, he was out. A brilliant thug who might have built a European community was defeated by a coalition dedicated to the sanctity and sovereignty of individual monarchies.

Throughout the 19th century statesmen devoted themselves to developing the states which sustained those monarchies or the republics that came to replace a few of them. Language, education, traditions both ancient and newly minted, all were used to increase people's sense of identification with the state and with its leaders.[11] These things helped distinguish each country from its neighbour, which spoke a different language, recalled a different history and committed itself to rival traditions which more often than not were erected on the basis of old enmities and wars.

So the 19th century came to be the century of fulfilment for the territorial state, and by its end western Europe was composed of little else. The states were different from one another, rejoicing in their differences and concerned to differentiate themselves further from their neighbours. Although they acknowledged that most of their rulers were one another's cousins and that they were members of a wider community they called the Concert of Europe, they seem lucky, in retrospect, to have kept the peace for most of the century before 1914.

The pattern of territorial states, dominant in western Europe and largely coterminous with nations, gradually extended itself eastwards. Britain and France were its exemplars, and Cavour and Bismarck set about turning Italy and Germany into nations like them. Further to the east, the Habsburgs and the Romanovs embraced in their huge dominions collections of nationalities; but by the early 20th century the Austro-Hungarian and Russian Empires were beginning to look like aberrations. The First World War brought an end to both, and to the Kaiser's; and throughout central and eastern Europe, Woodrow Wilson's principles put new states in their place. They were intended as far as possible to correspond with nations, and although embittered, disenfranchised minorities defeated the ingenuity of the mapmakers, by 1920 almost everyone in Europe, east as well as west, belonged to a state organised on the most up-to-date 20th century principles.

All these countries saw themselves as the proprietors of the individual's loyalties. For the democracies the state was the self-evidently essential element in international life; and as they came to power Mussolini, Hitler and Franco elevated the cult of the state to the level of hysteria. When the world went to war again, most of the millions who fought in it believed they were fighting not for Axis or Alliance but for the country whose uniform they wore.

After the Second World War, men tried again to put universal principles in place beside the state. Motives were mixed: in part to save the world of states from the consequences of their exaggerations, in part to replace them by the higher and perhaps more benevolent power of the United Nations. There were people who believed that the United Nations Organisation could lead to world government and others who looked to it merely to save the world from a repetition of the excesses of nationalism. In its early years, expectations ran high. One way or another, it was going to change the world for the better.[12]

The birth of the United Nations was followed by the collapse of every empire except the Soviet. In Asia within ten years and in Africa within 20, in the Caribbean and in Oceania, states took their place. Some matched national or tribal groupings; where they did not, the political leaders made the best of things, with movements of populations, the imposition of the state on tribal societies and general agreement to let inherited colonial frontiers stand. The state, and the cult of the nation, extended right around the globe, till the United Nations embraced getting on for 200 members, each of them sovereign and each of them undertaking in their differing degrees the international and domestic functions of a state.

By the 1970s, therefore, nation-states covered most of the world; and in the 1990s, when the Soviet empire went the way of the British, Dutch and French, the process was complete. The Commonwealth of Independent States offered few attractions to set against older loyalties. Latvians and Georgians, Estonians, Azerbaijanis, Uzbeks and Ukrainians suddenly found themselves free to build states of their own on the ruins of their hated Soviet republics. The triumph of the territorial state as the world's key organisational unit seemed complete.

But as the concept and practice of the nation-state grew stronger, rival forces were at work. The growing complexity of life, the spread of international trade and the growth of technology, the demands of efficiency and an increasing sensibility all brought to birth institutions that bound states together and in limited ways prevailed over them. The horrors of the Battle of Solferino in 1859, for example, brought the Red Cross into existence, and with it a new check on *raison d'état* in international relations. The establishment of the Universal Postal Union brought a first formalisation of economic and technical cooperation across frontiers. When the nations took the first steps to regulate such matters as the working hours of women on an international basis, they gave both humanitarian considerations and a concern for competition crossborder expression. As the workers of the world began to organise themselves internationally they recognised both their common humanity and the greater effectiveness which unity could bring them. The forces of civilisation, in short, were taking international as well as national form.

Each such development set some limit to the autarchy of the territorial state and created loyalties and identities which extended beyond it. Although in 1914 it was countries that went to war, asserting their national identity and their demands for unquestioning loyalty in the full panoply of Armageddon, there were already those who questioned the totally free expression of that authority. When, four years later, the horrors of war had exposed the shortcomings of nationalism, the world was ready for a more sophisticated essay at international relations. One of the many paradoxes of the 1918-21 settlements is the simultaneous extension of the national principle of organisation to the whole of Europe and the establishment of a League of Nations which set limits to the fullness of its expression. And one of the many tragedies of the interwar period was the failure either to establish effective supranational mechanisms or to use traditional, nation-based methods of organisation to block the advance of totalitarianism along the road to a second war.

It is however the half century since the end of the Second World War that has seen the most sustained challenge to the primacy of nations. The United Nations itself has fallen tragically short of the expectations of its founders and of the demands that have been put upon it, but it remains a principal factor in all international calculation. Some of its specialised agencies have assumed the roles of the bodies which the 19th century pragmatically created and have evolved many more. Some have done better than others, and one or two have done well; for good or evil, each has created some focus of commitment.[13] In the developing world the World Bank has more economic clout than the development agency of any single industrialised country. The International Monetary Fund goes on reinventing itself, and the rules of the World Trade Organisation inhibit the excesses even of the United States, the most solipsistic of its members. World government is not on this century's agenda nor, almost certainly, the next's; but the concepts of world governance, reformulated in the report of Ingvar Carlsson's and Shridath Ramphal's commission on the subject[14] continue to drip upon the stone of the state system.

If world organisations tell, at best, a story of limited achievement, some regional organisations have in the last 50 years scored real successes. The European Community, become the European Union, is an unequivocal success. It has saved the Europeans from themselves, helped build prosperity, and given Europe the beginnings of a single voice in the world. In their differing degrees, other regional groupings are achievements too. Each serves and depends upon its member states; and each erodes a little of their salience. Each makes some call on the commitment of individuals, even if most of them still think of themselves primarily as citizens of the state which issues their passports. Regional groupings will continue to arrogate more powers to themselves, if only because the efficient conduct of the world's business demands that they should.

At the same time, most states are challenged from below, by subsidiary levels of organisation. Dissatisfied with the services the state delivers to them in an increasingly globalised world, individuals seek the comfort of narrower identities. Britain faces the challenge of Scottish nationalist sentiment: a force which may come to represent something more forceful and appealing than Britishness, and which could lead to the dissolution of the United Kingdom. Other countries face comparable problems: Canada that of Quebec, Spain the separatist ambitions of the Basque country, Belgium the division that runs through its very heart. In parts of eastern Europe and the former Soviet Union, such dissatisfactions turn murderous. Beside these discontents, which are driven by the search for smaller, more intimate national identities, there are also regional and municipal ones, the urge to get government off provincial backs and claw power back from the centre, to get decisions taken nearer to the local street corner and to dispense with layers of government.

$$\backsim$$

The history of the state and its competitors in the last two centuries has led, therefore, to a stand-off between the demands of the nation-state and the pretensions of other kinds of political organisation. Where does the future lead? There are no certainties, but these are my best guesses.[15]

First, the United Nations and its agencies will survive the attacks of their critics and their own mistakes and remain the indispensable instruments of global coordination. Western Europe, for all its uncertainties, will continue to move towards integration. Super-patriots will mount counter-attacks, but they will be defeated. And, given the powers of attraction of the European Union, western Europe will draw most of central and eastern Europe along in its wake. There will be no end to American exceptionalism, and the United States will be truly at ease only in contexts in which it remains pre-eminent; but even Americans will continue to see advantage in increasing global and regional cooperation. Japan and China will pursue their national self-interests, the one with gradually decreasing diffidence, the other with its traditional self-confidence and with occasional outbursts of paranoia. Both of them, and the other countries of east, south-east and south Asia, will increasingly assert an Asian identity to put beside the national. Like the Americans, the Asians too will be brought by the complexity of social and economic circumstance to recognise the advantages of cooperation and even some integration. So will the rest of the world. Patriots will go on drawing metaphorical lines in the metaphorical sand, beyond which lie further surrenders of power to sinister forces and foreigners. But the world's needs point down a road that leads away from the exclusive authority of the state as we have understood it in the last two centuries.

Judging the direction of change is easier than estimating its speed. In 1990 some believed that we would see within ten years a full-fledged if ill-defined New International Order. We judged then that the United Nations might at last be entering into its inheritance. Now it is bloodied by its failures. It will survive, because the world needs it, but it will only very slowly be able to increase its authority. The European Union has always advanced by fits and starts interrupted by long periods of near stagnation. There can be no certainty today about the speed with which it will pursue the commitment to "ever closer union" to its uncertain destination. My guess is that the pursuit will continue through the early years of the next century, but at a pace reduced by national reaction within the present 15 and by the difficulties presented by enlargement to the east.

The prospects for Britain itself are equally hazy. The next chapter looks at its position and prospects. It gives no grounds for certainty that the United Kingdom will remain either united or a kingdom: Scotland feels itself a distinct nation, potentially capable of reversing the Act of Union, and all four countries nurture grievances which could rupture Britain's fabled continuity. Even if they do not demand revolutionary political change, the British people and their attitude towards their country will continue to change. Social change has produced attitudes and a social mix scarcely predictable in the 1960s, and the same process will bring more surprises in the first decades of the next century.

But it seems much more likely than not that for the next 25 years there will continue to be a Britain more or less recognisable in today's terms. Scotland will not become a separate, sovereign northern state like Denmark, and Northern Ireland will not evaporate into a united Ireland. Britain will remain an independent country, gradually becoming more committed to European integration and international cooperation. Early in that quarter-century it will lose the pound sterling, and with it some of its remaining limited freedom of economic action. At some point it may lose its Security Council seat but it will continue to play an important part in the world's game. Britain will, in short, retain most of its international characteristics, but in a form more attenuated than today's. There will still be a place called Britain and a people called the British, to take their place in a world of states, though states altered and hollowed out by forces that already challenge them.

1   Expressions used by Michael Ignatieff and Amitai Etzioni in "Concepts of Identity in the Twentieth Century", BBC Radio 4, 27 March 1996.
2   Ernst B Haas, *Beyond the Nation State* (Stanford: Stanford University Press, 1964).
3   Robert B Reich, *The Work of Nations* (London: Simon & Schuster, 1991).
4   Jean-Jacques Servan-Schreiber, *The American Challenge* (London: Hamish Hamilton, 1968).
5   Peter Willetts (ed.), *The Conscience of the World* (London: Hurst, 1996).
6   For an exhaustive examination of the interrelationship between individuals, states and security see Barry Buzan, *People, States and Fear, An Agenda for International Security Studies in the Post Cold-War Era* (Hemel Hempstead: Harvester, 1991).
7   For the process in Britain see Simon Jenkins, *Accountable to None* (London: Hamish Hamilton, 1995).
8   Alan Milward, *The European Rescue of the Nation State* (London: Routledge, 1992).
9   Douglas Hurd, *The Search for Peace* (London: Little Brown, 1997).
10 On this as other aspects of European history see Norman Davies, *Europe: A History* (Oxford: Oxford University Press, 1996).
11 Eric Hobsbawm and Terence Ranger (eds), *The Invention of Tradition* (Cambridge: Cambridge University Press, 1983).
12 Rosemary Righter, *Utopia Lost: The United Nations and World Order* (New York: Twentieth Century Fund, 1995).
13 Douglas Williams, *The Specialized Agencies and the United Nations* (London: Hurst, 1987).
14 *Our Global Neighbourhood, The Report of the Commission on Global Governance* (Oxford: Oxford University Press, 1995).
15 For a detailed survey of the world's prospects see Hamish McRae, *The World in 2020* (London: HarperCollins, 1994).

2   Europe's largest island

To a geographer, the United Kingdom is a state which occupies most of a group of islands just off the north-west coast of Europe. Ethnographically, its peoples are overwhelmingly the heirs of successive historic immigrations from the continent, supplemented in recent centuries by immigrants from further afield. To the historian they are people who have had more than their share of luck over the centuries and have made a disproportionate impact on the world. To the sociologist, Britain is a complex, predominantly urban society. To an economist it is an industrial and post-industrial state, dependent to an unusual degree on foreign trade and investment. To a psychologist Britishness is a state of mind, based on a vast range of experiences in common.

This sense of Britishness competes with other identities for attention. Historically, it is a parvenu: Chaucer and Shakespeare were Englishmen, Burns a Scotsman, and the peoples of these islands thought of themselves as English or Welsh, Irish or Cornish or Scottish, centuries before their 18th- and 19th-century rulers told them that they were British.[1] For some, more local loyalties endure – to Essex, Yorkshire, Liverpool or the Borders. So does identification by class, a little bashful today but almost as powerful as it has ever been. Employment or lack of it makes a critical mark. Roman Catholicism remains a badge, and not just in Northern Ireland. So does Jewry. This century's immigrants have brought with them obvious ethnic distinctions. Age too makes a difference, in terms both of present preference and past experience. There are individual Britons with a deep conviction that they belong in society, and equally convinced outsiders. Some are addicted to John

Major's warm beer, others to Ecstasy.

Then there are psychological commitments that extend beyond national boundaries. For many Britons there is a growing identification with other Europeans, whether for Beethoven's sake, business advantage or the sunshine of Mediterranean holidays. Many others identify still with kith and kin in the old Commonwealth, or with a United States seen as Britain's natural friend. For some, Zionism plucks at heart strings, as families and memories in the Caribbean do for others. There is a commitment to overseas charity, to the poor of the earth. There are Britons who believe in world government or the indivisibility of humanity or a United States of Europe. Many of these convictions coexist with a sense of a primary commitment to Britain; others contradict it; all diminish it as a singular expression of identity.

In the years since the Second World War the British people have indulged themselves in an orgy of introspection, dissatisfied with what is and looking for something better. But they are not a revolutionary people and for Britain this is not an era of catastrophe. There is no very powerful reason for the British people to abandon their Britishness in what is left of this century or in the early decades of the next. Nevertheless, a psychiatrist would tell us that in the last 20 years at least there has been something fraught about this sense of Britishness. It came with a conviction that Britain is not as important, successful, efficient or even as worthy as it once was, and as its people would like it to be. It is a conviction that has infected Britons' attitudes to other countries also, to the world at large, and to where Britain belongs in it.

In 1997 there was some reduction in this unease, some recovery of national nerve and self-confidence. We have experienced this before, in a burst of national self-confidence in the 1980s that did not last. The results of Labour's election victory may prove more enduring, but only a confirmed gambler would put much money on it. At a deeper level, the feeling of inadequacy has not yet been exorcised. Its origins and justifications deserve close examination, but it is of its very nature a subjective and partial thing. Evaluation is difficult, but it is worth a try.

～

We might start by looking at the statistics. With 58 million people,

Britain is the 20th most populous country in the world. In Europe it comes fifth, just behind France and ahead of Italy. There are more than enough Britons for healthy disagreements about the state of their country and about where it belongs. And in terms of area the little offshore island is not so little: getting on for 250,000 square kilometres, the 12th largest country in Europe.

Conventional measurement makes the British economy the fifth largest in the world, behind the United States, Japan, Germany and France. Correction for a distortion familiar to economists puts China and India ahead of Britain, with Britain in eighth place. But Britain remains the world's fifth largest exporter of goods and the fourth largest exporter of invisibles. Add to this economic underpinning Britain's political, military and intellectual resources, and the country emerges as a middling-sized member of Global United's First Eleven.

In terms of wealth per head, however, Britain ranks 22nd (or 17th if you strip out special instances like Luxembourg, Iceland and the United Arab Emirates). The listing puts Britain in the 11th place in the European Union, ahead only of Ireland, Spain, Portugal and Greece, well behind the Germans and French whom the British see as their natural equals, and behind even the Italians. Whether you see this as matter for alarm or as a natural consequence of national predilections persisted in over decades is a matter of taste. To an envoy from Mars on a two-day visit there is nothing particularly terrible, or disgraceful, about being the 22nd richest people in the world.[2]

But earthly mortals compare such figures with the past and project them into the future. It is a fact that over the past 30 years almost all of western Europe has caught up with and overtaken Britain in terms of average economic well-being. Italy rejoiced when it surpassed the United Kingdom as an economic power. So, famously and by a much bigger margin, did Japan. Hong Kong and Singapore have a higher GDP per head than Britain, and − financial convulsions permitting − Taiwan and South Korea will come along behind. As more countries of east Asia and the Pacific Rim come into their inheritance, Britain's comparative economic well-being is bound to slip further down the tables. And if relative economic weakness has a tendency to accelerate out of control, concerns about Britain's ability to hold on to the economic standards and comforts it enjoys today are justified.

Nevertheless, in absolute terms, the man from Mars would discover a prosperous place, delivering more wealth to more of its people than in any decade of its golden past. And wealth is matched by other blessings. Beneath all the blemishes and the abuses, Britain enjoys an estimable quality of democratic politics and peaceable social order, a decent legal system, efficient and accessible national and local administration and a fair degree of social cohesion. Our conclusion must be that by world standards in 1998, Britain is a reasonably comfortable place of residence for most of us.

⌐

Such a conclusion would have sat easily with the complacency that 19th-century visitors used to identify as Britain's most noticeable characteristic. More recent visitors, however, have found a very different country, one profoundly uneasy about itself, concerned with how it looks to others in a way quite alien to its more self-confident past.

Persistent self-critical introspection has set the tone for much of British life in the 1990s. How far was it and is it justified? It starts with the undeniable truth that Britain is globally far less important than it was. Observers were documenting decline compared with other countries in the second half of the last century, and by the early years of this one it was clear that Germany and the United States were formidable rivals to a country that still thought of itself, fairly accurately, as pre-eminent.[3] The First World War, fought to a victorious finish, nevertheless diminished Britain's position relative to the United States. Between the wars Britain failed to meet the challenge of the dictators until it was almost too late, and both Germany and Japan put into the field more formidable armed forces. The Second World War, bringing finest hour and cathartic fulfilment, spelt also the end of Britain's hopes of again exercising lasting global power.[4] After it, the recovery of France, Germany and Japan diminished further Britain's weight and importance, just as the emergence of new industrial powers is doing today.

The decline of political and military power was punctuated, and at times caused, by misjudgment and lack of political will. But its principal cause was a steady reduction of Britain's economic power. That decline was in one sense inevitable, as competitors industrialised in its wake, with 19th-century Belgium, Germany, the United States and France in turn creating the railway networks, the coalmines, the cotton mills and the ironworks on which Britain's lead had been based.[5] Britain's industrial capital aged, accelerated by the City of London's aptitude for investing British capital to maximum advantage abroad, enriching the political and property-owning classes but helping to make Britain a prematurely rentier state.[6] Social prejudice against business and technical educational failings also played their part.[7] Protectionism between the wars failed to check the process of decline, and the Second World War dramatically revealed the inadequacy of Britain's industrial base.[8] And when, after the war, economic argument spoke for industrial investment to recover the ground that had been lost, political and social predilection demanded investment in a world role and the welfare state instead.[9]

But decline, whether political or economic, is one thing. Failure is another. Since the 1950s at least, British political discourse has been instinct with a conviction of failure a well as decline. Gradually this sense has encompassed new areas of concern. In the 1960s and 1970s it was economic inefficiency that caused concern. This inevitably had psychological and social consequences, and Britain's failure as a wealth creator kept taxes at penal levels and limited the investment the country could make in socially desirable enterprises; but socially and politically the country believed itself to be sound. Gradually, however, that confidence evaporated too, and the concerns of the British body politic became as much constitutional, political and social as economic.

Where you place the blame for what many see as a chronicle of failure as well as decline is a matter of age and of political taste. There are still those who blame late imperial, global overstretch in the 1940s and 1950s for the condition of Britain today.[10] Others point to the creation of expectations of social welfare which put the cart before the horse and now, half a century later, must be confronted with painful reality.[11] Our social woes, in some eyes, stem from a liberal binge in the frivolous 1960s. It is hard to find anyone with a good word for the domestically lost years of the 1970s; and Britain's entry in 1973 into the European Community seems to some the beginning of all evil as to others it is the beginning of wisdom. In the 1980s, as few of us will forget, Britain made a convulsive effort under Margaret Thatcher which put some critically important economic matters right but seemed – perhaps most dramatically in the poll tax riots – to stretch the country's social cohesion to breaking point, leaving new weaknesses for the politics of the 1990s to grapple with.

&

The British conviction that they were failures pervaded their attitudes to politics, society and economics. Whether they were right or wrong is perhaps beside the point. "History," Felipe Fernandez-Armesto tells us, "is littered with the debris of empires whose peoples talked themselves into decline."[12] If the British have made their own talkative contribution to their decline over the last half century, are they doomed to go on doing so? Can they, by taking thought, check the process ? Can they even, as successive political leaders urge them, gather their courage around them and start to recover some of the ground that they have lost ? What should we be doing differently ? What changes in our national arrangements would make Britain a more successful, self-confident, happier place?

These are questions for each individual Briton to answer for himself. But every politician and most commentators have answers of their own, and they propound ways in which Britain could, if it would, check the process of decline. Most of the problem is domestic, and so their proposals address primarily domestic concerns. But each has implications for Britain's overseas position; and the issue which provokes the shrillest disagreements of all, Europe, weaves the threads of domestic and international concern into one cloth.

Constitutional doubts come first, because constitutional arrangements affect every other aspect of society. It was in this field that complacency endured longest, but it does so no longer. The monarchy is on the run, and its troubles interact with other issues, such as the future of the Union of the four countries and of the European Union. We could live to see the United Kingdom become a republic, conceivably a federal republic, and many already hope for it. But it seems more likely than not that the monarchy will survive. It was slow to recognise the necessity for reform, and remote and unimaginative in its efforts to respond to a fundamental shift in the nation's attitude. Individual folly could still bring it to its knees, but more probably a chastened monarchy will lead the country through the early decades of the next century. It will not take too much ingenuity to reconcile monarchy with Celtic discontents and with whatever European integration the future brings; it can help hold the Commonwealth together, if the members want it to; and at home it can give us the decent representational services of more modest, Scandinavian-style kings and queens.[13]

Demands for a more formalised constitutional structure than the sovereignty of queen in parliament are less likely to go away.[14] The British have lost patience with woolly-minded empiricism. Well-meaning foreigners remind them that something in the air, or their intellectual formation, deters them from rigorous conceptual thought. Their history has denied them the incentive and the means to adapt their constitutional arrangements to changes in society. Now they feel they need a constitution which responds to the assertion of the individual's rights and the rejection of a pre-ordained place in a social pecking order.[15] It must guarantee individual rights against the state and against the corporate world, Celtic and other national rights against Westminster, and English rights against Celtic favouritism. A reshaped Upper House can play a part in defending all these interests.

But constitutional change alone will not restore the authority of politicians. A government 18 years in power learned bad habits of arrogance and irresponsibility. Even if it had resisted them, the decline of deference would have stolen much of the politicians' wardrobe. Society has learned to hold them responsible for Britain's failure to cope with changing circumstances, and their short-term opportunism has lent substance to the charge.[16] In 1997 the new Labour government brought a change of style which already, a year later, is beginning to fray at the edges. Whoever is in power, party commitment caricatures the essentially confrontational nature of too many British institutions such as the law, the press and an Oxbridge education. Television shows the viewer what looks like the irrelevance of Parliament's everyday doings and at the same time provides a more effective forum for questioning ministers about their deeds. Brussels has usurped much of Westminster's authority. The necessary trade of politics is out of favour and unfashionable.

Against that, there persists a lively interest in political issues, manifested in television viewing, the broadsheet newspapers and the saloon bar. The British people believe that they own their politics as few of their European neighbours do. They still seem eager to give Tony Blair and the Labour Party the benefit of the doubt. If that continues, Labour will have a chance to bring revived authority to politics, but with its vast majority it will need self-discipline if it is not to go the overbearing and in the end disastrous way of the last administration.

Whilst they have been losing natural authority, government and politics have sucked formal authority out of other institutions. Since 1979 Quangos, accountable only to ministers, have usurped much of the ground that used to be local government's.[17] The civil service today is more cost-conscious and businesslike than it was, but it has been diminished as a force for objectivity beside government. It is now a less effective check on ministers' doings than it should be.[18] Similarly, the judges have made no secret of their concern that ministers are stealing their discretion. We need to beware of the complaints of those who see their authority diminished by measures to shake up complacent institutions. All the same, the destruction or depreciation of so many institutions which stood between government and people was a strange legacy for a Conservative administration which proclaimed that it was dedicated to attacking Big Government. In early 1998 there are hopes that Labour will do better, but signs already that it too is tempted by the delights of centralised authority.

Nor is Britain as economically liberal a society as the last government would have had it. Health, safety and environmental regulations still proliferate, in part in response to European Union rules, in part to government's own perception of the demands of an increasingly complex and technical society. So does financial regulation, pinning the wings of a City that believes it should fly free, earning more for Britain than industry ever will. There are arguments for regulation as there are for deregulation, and some would say that the BSE catastrophe is a timely reminder of the dangers of letting market forces decide things that lie beyond their ken. It is a fact that as modern industrial nations go, particularly outside Europe, Britain is not a particularly unregulated society. This is going to be an issue that divides British politics, and yet another topic on which the pros and cons of commitment to the

European Union will get involved with domestic disagreements.

~

In the past 15 years, concern about all these things has been added to preoccupation with the competitiveness of the economy. To most observers, this is the field in which Britain has been most successful in improving its performance. The defence of unsustainable exchange rates is a thing of the past, at least until we start to shadow the euro. Overweening union power has gone. So very largely has incompetent management. Along with the rest of the industrial world we have tamed inflation. We have stopped losing international market share. We export like professionals; we invest effectively abroad; we are quick, or fairly quick, to seek out new markets. Compared with many of our competitors, particularly in Europe, our economy – strong on services, relatively high-tech, information-based – looks to the future rather than the past. So it is a fair generalisation that industrially and economically Britain is truly stronger than it was 20 years ago. To a continental European businessman, its economy looks enviably free, flexible and responsive. To the Japanese and the Americans, it has for decades been the best place in Europe to invest.

But the price Britain paid to break out of its economic decline was high, and many of the consequences are with us still: a shrunken industrial base, insecurity in work, unemployment which is historically high if low by comparison with many of our partners, and by some measures the worst extremes of poverty and inequality in any western European nation. The year-on-year economic decline that for long seemed inexorable has been broken. But whether Britain can hold on to these costly gains is an open question. It leads us straight into Britain's choices about its place in the world.

In most fields, Britain is today competitive in Europe. If it chooses to commit itself whole-heartedly to the European Union, it has today the economic muscle to back up that commitment: industrially one of Europe's big four, agriculturally competitive, pre-eminent in services and head and shoulders above the rest in financial services. But the European Union is not the only benchmark, and much of the rest of the world is driving forward faster than the Europeans. In the last ten years the United States has reasserted an economic pre-eminence it had seemed to be losing. Japan, having come from nowhere in half a century, seems checked: the check may be temporary or permanent, but Japan has made itself and will remain an economic power more comparable with the United States than with any single European country. In time the new Asian industrialised countries will bounce back from their present financial troubles, just as China will continue its march to power. Much of the developing world is stirring. These are the realities which provoke the rejoinder that Europe, and competitiveness in Europe, is not enough. They also provoke the suggestion, in part well-founded, in part fanciful, that of all the European countries Britain is the best placed to take advantage of opportunities in the more fluid world outside Europe.

Britain's overseas choices are matters for later chapters. But the fight to become, or to remain, competitive in international terms raises other domestic issues. The most central is the question of investment in intellectual and industrial capital. What educational and technological training reforms are needed to fit young Britons for the modern workplace, and how do we put effective investment behind them there?

In the 1997 election the voters gave overwhelming support to Labour's commitment to put more resources into education, technology and investment. In doing so, they endorsed a reaction against reliance on both market forces and business judgment which, for 18 Conservative years, had improved economic performance but had failed to give Britain a modern, internationally competitive productive base.[19] And the country faces the same choice in its external alignment, between the social market economic approach of the European countries and the free market, buccaneering ways of Asia and the United States. Here, once again, foreign and domestic preoccupations interlock.

International comparisons get into discussion of the nation's social choices also. There was a time when the British believed rightly that their welfare state and health service were models for the world. Now they believe that most of western Europe has moved ahead of them. But demographic change, job insecurity and the costs of modern medicine confront all industrialised countries with choices more pressing than that between Scandinavian or Iberian standards of social welfare.

Can Britain and most other European countries any longer afford the welfare standards of the best of them? Do they want to pay their price in taxes? Can their industries, hard pressed by American and Asian competition, carry the social costs of European standards of welfare?

Listening to the arguments on both sides of this debate, to the case for compassion and the case for competitiveness, it would be nice to be able to opt for both. There are sceptics who will tell you that Labour's subliminal message is that we can. But it is not just confrontational politics that demands a choice. So do the logic and the political psychology inherent in the two approaches. So does the fact that resources invested in higher education are resources that cannot be put into tax cuts calculated to motivate the wealth creators to create more. The nation made a clear choice between the parties at the 1997 election, but the parties themselves had fudged – and still fudge – the underlying issues.

⌒

A common thread runs through most of these political and social concerns. Individual Britons have always been haunted by one aspect or another of insecurity: the threat of unemployment, unwanted pregnancy, street violence, an impoverished old age. But now insecurity troubles almost all of us. It self-evidently afflicts the underclass and the unemployed. It threatens also those in work, whose confidence about their worth and about the future is undermined by sweeping change in the shape and structure of employment. The self-employed middle classes, their numbers enhanced by those who have lost old, familiar employments, are in their own way as unsure of the future as are the unemployed. So are all those who fret about the National Health Service, or take out private health insurance to escape from it. They see that the welfare state can do less for them than it did and they fear that authority is no longer concerned to ensure that there are no holes in the safety net. The old, inevitably, feel vulnerable, and, like Britain's minorities, particularly its black minorities, feel particularly exposed to the lawlessness and crime which seem to have taken possession of the streets. And there is now little confidence in the law enforcers, even among the middle classes.

An abused natural world adds to this sense of insecurity. Ever since the Chernobyl reactor explosion, we have feared the disasters that science causes or cannot check. AIDS, BSE, an unknown plague in Africa, all haunt us. So do threats of global warming and holes in the ozone layer. The consequences of the abuse of our environment and of animals are campaigning issues. There is a sense, unscientific but profound for all that, that mankind has flown too near the sun.

Insecurity is an international disease, and Britain's version is not yet acute by world standards. But the British, looking back to an age when their security seemed golden, feel a particular vulnerability by comparison with that past. This sense of insecurity about the future has come to stand beside a sense of failure about the past. It is certain to remain a central concern of British politics.

∽

Let us return to our envoy from Mars. He might report on his flying visit to Britain as follows.

• Britain is one of the world's most prosperous and secure countries. Its people still mourn past greatness and are only gradually coming to terms with their decline. This imbues them with a largely unjustified sense of national failure, which they are only slowly shaking off.

• There is no objective reason why Britain should not make itself a happier place. To do so will need nerve and self-discipline. The British must learn to love their neighbour and rediscover the art of disciplined discourse. They must erode the traditional differences that divide people by class and interest group, and beware of those who seek to create new antagonisms. They must build a politics that is creative and constructive. They need to create a system of education that delivers the results that the turn-of-the-century world demands. And if they are to hold on to their comfortable prosperity they must work hard and compete cleverly in a global market.

• Most of the problems that obsess the British are domestic ones, but in today's world domestic issues are inseparable from international ones. Britain has an important position in the world that serves its own, and the world's, best interests. But Britain is changing. So is the world. The British need to accept that autonomy is a fantasy and to decide afresh where in that world they belong. For their sense of themselves, and therefore their happiness, depends largely on their relationship with the other inhabitants of Planet Earth.

1 Linda Colley, *Britons. Forging the Nation 1707–1837* (London: Pimlico, 1992).

2 For these and later rankings see *The Economist Pocket World in Figures,* 1998 edition (London: Profile Books, 1997).

3 Eric Hobsbawm, *The Age of Empire* (London: Weidenfeld & Nicolson, 1987).

4 David Childs, *Britain Since 1939. Progress and Decline* (London: Macmillan, 1995).

5 Eric Hobsbawm, *The Age of Revolution* (London: Weidenfeld & Nicolson, 1975).

6 P J Cain and A G Hopkins, *British Imperialism. Innovation and Expansion, 1688–1914* (London: Longman, 1993).

7 David Coates and John Hillard (eds), *The Economic Decline of Modern Britain* (Brighton: Wheatsheaf, 1986).

8 Corelli Barnett, *The Audit of War* (London: Macmillan, 1986).

9 For Britain's economic decline in the context of its international competitivity see Michael E Porter, *The Competitive Advantage of Nations* (London: Macmillan, 1990); and for discussion of the reasons see Peter Clark and Clive Trebilcock (eds). *Understanding Decline : Perceptions and Realities of British Economic Performance* (Cambridge: Cambridge University Press, 1997).

10 For the issues set in a global context see Paul Kennedy, *The Rise and Fall of the Great Powers* (New York: Random House, 1987).

11 Barnett, *op. cit.*

12 Felipe Fernandez-Armesto, *Millennium* (London: Bantam Press, 1995).

13 Jim Northcott, *Britain in 2010* (London: Policy Studies Institute, 1991).

14 For an up-to-date if partisan view see Anthony Barnett, *This Time* (London: Vintage, 1997).

15 Foreshadowed by L A Siedentop in "Viewpoint: the strange life of liberal England", *Times Literary Supplement*, 16 August 1985.

16 Andrew Marr, *Ruling Britannia* (London: Michael Joseph, 1995).

17 Simon Jenkins, *Accountable to None* (London: Hamish Hamilton, 1995).

18 Peter Hennessy, *Whitehall* (London: Fontana, 1989).

19 Will Hutton, *The State We're In* (London: Jonathan Cape, 1995).

3   The islanders look at the world

The British think of themselves as an unemotional people who shy away from gestures and heroics and are driven by practical considerations. The political classes believe that their conduct of foreign relations is governed by their heads, not by their hearts or by unrealistic ambitions. Hence the pride they take in Palmerston's exaltation of British interests above Britain's allies.[1] The fact that there is much historical evidence to the contrary leaves the judgment unaffected. The British are emotionally and ideologically committed to the belief that they are unemotional and strangers to ideology. They have the same conviction as the fat man who thinks that he is thin or the pretty girl who is convinced that she is plain.

They display a similar emotionalism when they turn their minds to foreigners. Hence a distrust of Germans that lingers a whole generation after continental Europeans say they have put most of their suspicions behind them.[2] Hence too their ambivalence about the French, neighbours, rivals and sparring partners for a millennium: the British simultaneously despise and admire the French, view them with distrust and admire them as Europe's only true sophisticates.[3] The same emotionalism pervades British attitudes towards the developing world, as aroused by "tin-pot tyrants" as by the sufferings of the poor. The British distinguish themselves even from people very like themselves, as when Prince Charles dismisses the Scandinavian monarchies as stuffy. Emotionalism ties the British in knots again in their feelings about the United States, despising Americans as materialists, admiring them as a nation of unbounded expectations, desiring above all that they should admire us for something more than country pubs and cottages with honeysuckle round the door.

These emotions are of course mixed up with calculation, the beady eye to self-interest in which the British take such pride, leading to cross-purposes, and too often the hypocrisy which foreigners profess to believe is the true mark of Albion. When an issue bores the British people, they allow professional calculation to prevail over emotion. But when their attention is engaged, so will their emotions be, as they have been whenever in history Britain has found itself confronted with great challenges or opportunities.

Britain's history has been shaped by its geography, which placed it on the very edge of Europe, near enough to fall victim to Romans, Angles, Vikings and Normans in turn, and near enough to provide it with continental standards of comparison ever afterwards.[4] Location also affected the attitudes of the English to others. So they defined themselves firstly in terms of their differences from other Europeans. At the same time, at least part of the self-definition of the Scots, Irish and Welsh turned on their differences from their English neighbours, who became for the Scots perennial enemies and for the Welsh and Irish, conquerors.

Yet for a millennium all four peoples were defined also by membership of the Universal Church. Catholicism was something in common between them and the peoples of the continent. The Church's business brought Augustine to England and took bold Irish missionaries to the Germans. The monasteries of the British Isles were part of a network that spread across all of Europe from Monte Cassino to Jervaulx. The master builders and journeyman sculptors who created Winchester and Salisbury worked also on the cathedrals of France and Flanders.

There were secular links also. For 300 years the English imported their claret from vintners who, like them, owed allegiance to the English crown. Between Franco-English wars, kings of England contracted Franco-English marriages. They felt for France or Burgundy or Spain as much sympathy or animosity as they felt for Scotland. Meanwhile the Scots cultivated their alliance with their neighbour's neighbour. Between the English and the Scots and the continentals there was a sense of affinity as well as difference. Chaucer's pilgrims had heard tales of the continent, its languages and peoples, of Santiago de Compostela as well as Canterbury. Beside familiarity the islanders cherished a sense of difference: of the Channel in between, of an English language growing in importance beside French and Latin, of a distinct society shaped by the interplay between Normans and Anglo-Saxons. But the differences were contained within the cloak of an undivided Christendom.

The Renaissance brought the peoples of the British Isles reminders of the classical origins and cultural roots they had in common with their European neighbours. But it also brought the more effective authority and administration of modernising kings. The Tudors defined nationality with a precision earlier kings had not. In England and Scotland, as elsewhere, the idea of the nation as an affinity group, distinguished from outsiders not just by loyalties to its ruler but also by specific characteristics of its own, was conceived. Henry VII and Henry VIII meant something different to the English people from their predecessors. They also meant something different to England's neighbours.[5]

The late Renaissance saw the death of the Universal Church. The sixteenth-century prince chose his church and most of his people followed. Henry VIII's breach with Rome destroyed the old textures of English religious life, putting in their place a national religious system which set England apart from France and Spain. This rejection of the papacy, of the monastic orders and the old ways would alone have added a religious element to an English sense of separateness. Mary's counter-revolution and Elizabeth's settlement reinforced it. Fears of the Counter-Reformation and above all Spain completed the process of setting a real difference between England and her greatest rivals.

Religion set the Scottish and the Irish apart from the English. In Scotland, Calvinism created a society very different from its own past and from its English neighbour. And Ireland's loyalty to the old faith introduced yet another element of difference and friction between the Irish, their English rulers and Scottish settlers. Thus the four peoples of the British Isles were different from one another and different from the peoples of the continent. But gradually English, Scots, Protestant Irish and Welsh came to recognise affinities and interests in common. The limited sense of Britishness thrived on a diet of difference from outsiders. The process led to an acceptance of the reality which became the United Kingdom.[6] At the same time it created animosities, so that from the 16th century to the 1790s, Britain's relations with the continent were shaped by its continuing wars with Their Most Catholic and Most Christian Majesties of Spain and France.

∽

Britain's dealings with the continent have their roots in ten centuries of history. But from the 16th century onwards geography was involving the country in a quite different historical saga, unmarked by the ambivalence which dogged relationships with the continent. Geography gave the people of the British Isles access to the Atlantic and the seas of the world. They went to sea as pirates and explorers, slavers, settlers, conquerors and missionaries, creating a worldwide network of settlements and connections which persists today, 30 years after the end of empire. And they planted in stay-at-home British minds two equally persistent views of the world.[7]

The first is a fruit of settlement, of the colonies planted in the Americas and the Antipodes. To this day the British consider Americans, Canadians and Antipodeans to be qualitatively different from other foreigners. They extended the same courtesy to English-speaking South Africans and white Rhodesians. The attitude outlived the American Revolution and the loss of the first British empire. Alliances in two wars reinforced it. It ignores the changes which later immigration has wrought in the composition of the American, Canadian and Australian peoples – and, for that matter, of British society itself. It is intensely dated now and its most convinced adherents are ageing. But it still has its relevance, as we shall see when we come to examine Britain's relationships with the United States, and the possibility of breathing new life into the Commonwealth.

The second view of the world derives from conquest and exploitation, which have bequeathed to today's Britons a sense of guilt and complacency, intimacy and distinction, love and hate with most of the developing world. When the British conquered a quarter of the globe they found most of it occupied already. India showed them a culture grander and older than their own, set beside extreme poverty, corruption and oppression. Africa confronted them with tribal societies quite unable to stand against their civilisation. They made the West Indies fertile through the labour of slaves, and in the Pacific they discovered an untouched island world.[8] They made the same kind of discoveries outside the lands they colonised – in China, the Levant, South America and the spice islands of the East Indies.

The British dealt with all these societies with an absolute conviction of superiority. They did much good and much harm, and for better or for worse permanently changed the conditions of life of most of those with whom they came in contact. They started the process of integrating these places, hitherto largely unknown to the West, into a kind of world order, defined by administration and driven by trade.

It was that system which made possible the transformation of Britain into the world's first industrial power. It gave individual Britons of every estate opportunities to live, work and fight overseas, and to discover societies totally different from their own. Whereas the overseas settlements gave those who remained at home the sense that they had cousins and friends in distant places, rule over subject races brought home to the British an awareness and some understanding of peoples even more different from them than the continental Europeans. If there is such a thing as a functioning British diaspora, extending all the way from screen writers in Hollywood to aid workers in Rwanda and market speculators in Singapore, it has its origins in the empire.

The relationship with India and the colonies made its mark within Britain also. In the beginning it was little more than a matter of curiosity: the rare emancipated slave, the occasional visitor, the curious Asian or African artefact. But the inflows, both of people and things, increased: tea in the 18th century, industry-creating cotton in the early 19th, a steadily increasing number of Indian traders and Chinese seamen later in the century. By the early 20th century, Britain was ceasing to be an exclusively white-faced society, and in the 1960s immigrants from the Caribbean, East Africa and the subcontinent started to make it a multi-ethnic one. As the flow increased, barriers to immigration went up; but any generalisation about Britain's place in the world has to take account of the 6 per cent or so of its population of Asian, African and Caribbean origin whose presence is perhaps the most enduring reminder of the empire that has gone.

These twin realities, the close but different continent and the British presence around the globe, came into sharp political and military focus in the wars against the French Revolution and Napoleon.[9] From 1789 to 1815 Britain fought almost uninterruptedly against France and much of the continent. These campaigns took British armies into the Low Countries and to the Caribbean, to the Baltic and Spain, and finally to Waterloo. The Royal Navy ranged to the Nile and the West Indies, to Copenhagen and Trafalgar, and British cruisers and privateers quartered the oceans. British finance supported the armies of half Europe and British blockade runners pitted themselves against Napoleon's Continental System. At the end of it all Britannia was confirmed as the ruler of the waves, the world's pre-eminent political and industrial power.[10]

The contest profoundly affected British attitudes towards the rest of the world. It added another element to the Britons' sense that their European enemies were different: first a revolutionary people in arms, then regicides and terrorists, and finally the servants of a tyrant intent on dominating Europe. Britain had fought before to preserve a balance of power between the European monarchies, but the war against Napoleon brought to fulfilment the doctrine that Britain could not afford to see any single power dominate the continent. The world wars against the French also reinforced the conviction that Britain had business and interests everywhere. They provided the most graphic evidence of the superiority of God's Englishman: the evidence of victory.

From the end of the wars in 1815, Great Britain was what diplomatic historians used to call a satisfied power. The British had problems to resolve at home: poverty, industrialisation, Ireland, the vote. But abroad, secure in possession of the Royal Navy, a global trading system and the world's most developed industrial base, they could afford to be complacent, to become benevolent and sanctimonious and patronising while they snapped up in Africa the last constituents of empire. In Harold Nicolson's words, "We could afford the luxury of gentleness because we were completely unafraid". Of course there is far more to Britain's 19th-century history than that: the horrors of the Crimea and the Indian Mutiny, the war scares in Europe and the opium wars in China. But the 19th century brought to full flower the ideas about foreign parts which were germinated in the British mind in earlier centuries.

The 19th century also produced the first warning signs that the idyll would not continue unchallenged for ever. The United States and Germany began to present industrial competition, and after the American Civil War and the Franco-Prussian War they posed potential military challenges also. To the Victorians Russia was a threat to India, and across the Channel France remained the historical enemy. Many things nagged away at British anxieties: not just the growth in German power, but German social welfare and educational advances, which contrasted so starkly with the neglect of the British working class; unrest in India; a sense of political and military over-extension; occasional defeat and sudden death in unconsidered colonial wars. The Boer War demonstrated the sheer difficulty of the imperial balancing act and the resentment it evoked in Europe. America and Germany were building battle fleets. But above all, Britain's industrial base was ageing, absolutely as old investment wore out and too much new investment went overseas; and relatively, as the Americans and the continentals closed the gap between our achievements and theirs.[11]

෴

We saw in the last chapter that this sense that others were overtaking us, beginning in the late 19th century and accelerating in the 20th, has been an essential element in sapping the confidence of the British about themselves. It has also infected British thinking about the outside world. Country, crown and empire came triumphantly through the First World War as other empires and dynasties crumbled. At the end of it Britain was prominent, perhaps pre-eminent, among the victors. But it had seen the Germans organised for war and the Americans coming in, unbloodied, in their millions. Between the wars the totalitarians half-persuaded Britain that they stood for the future in contrast to the effete democracies. And the second war convinced the British of the detailed reality of decline.

The Soviet Union and the United States won the Second World War. Britain counted itself among the victors, but the war had wrung out of it the essentials of great power status. Overseas wealth was gone, domestic industrial capacity diminished. Britain's overseas possessions turned first from assets into liabilities, and then went their way to independence. The two superpowers simply outweighed the British. And gradually the various recoveries of the defeated – France, Italy, Germany and Japan – began to impinge on the British mind.

The British know a few things about the relative success of their rivals. By most measures of economic success Germany had by the 1960s overtaken Britain and begun to build a quietly good society. The 1990s brought the opportunity to integrate the eastern *Länder*, a process which will take decades but which already makes of Germany a giant of over 80 million people. British suspicions of Germany run deep, but they are partnered by an unaffectionate admiration. France, too, has contrived its economic miracle, surpassing Britain today by most measures by 20 per cent. Even Italy, a country riven by political and social ills, can boast that it has overtaken Britain economically. And the British know that only four countries in the whole European Union are worse off than they are. They read across from their neighbours' economic success and see in them other virtues: in Germany deep industrial strengths, in France an enviable national self-confidence, in Spain a dramatic resurgence and in Italy a capacity for muddling through which we once thought uniquely our own.

Japan presents the British with the same problems of acceptance as Germany, but in spades: the second defeated enemy which has done so much better than Britain out of the peace. Their diverse attitudes towards the Japanese suffer from their inability to integrate them. They admire Japan's industrial ingenuity and covet the products which it produces. They welcome Japanese investment more successfully than other Europeans and take to the industrial culture of Japanese companies like ducks to water. Yet they nurse folk memories of wartime atrocities and see in Japanese domestic life a rabbit-hutch inhumanity. They know that the Japanese are ruthless whalers and drift-netters, careless of animal welfare and brutally abusive of their Korean minority. Until they are taught better they even imagine that the most expensive country in the world is defeating them with sweated labour.

East Asia's present troubles bring us passing *Schadenfreude* but we know that they mar rather than negate great strengths. The South Koreans have their problems, but in two decades they have come from nowhere to invest in Britain and sell us cars with unpronounceable names. Hong Kong and Singapore have overtaken us in wealth per head. Malaysia has notched up spectacular rates of economic growth yet still cherishes sour resentments of British colonialism, made the sourer recently by its own financial and environmental troubles. Above all, we sense China's immanent capacity to put capitalism and millions of productive workers at the service of authoritarian nationalism. Our understanding of what is happening in Asia is imperfect, but we sense that it will change the world. Our minds tell us that east Asia represents opportunity, but to head and heart alike it represents a problem also; and our emotions tell us that the best thing about the post-Confucian world is that it is very far away.

In south Asia, India is at last setting its economy free and may lead its neighbours out of poverty. Investors, exporters and diplomats see opportunities, and a chance to use connections inherited from imperial times to seize them. But to the Briton in the street, south Asia is still a part of the world's problems, not its opportunities, a part of that great swathe of the South which we call developing and privately think of as hopeless. The images of the subcontinent that linger in the mind are of beggars and child labourers, human rights abuses in Pakistan and disastrous cyclones in Bangladesh. These are the images which still arouse the mixture of revulsion and guilt which the British learned when they colonised the world. Those who are professionally involved in the developing world know better. But the rest of us still see it through a distorting prism, held up to view by aid agencies and reporters of famine and catastrophe, by exiles agitating against tyrants, and by old men who once planted coffee in Kenya or tea in the Assam hills.

One aspect of what we used to think of as the third world faces the British with a different kind of problem. There was a time when they thought they had a special empathy with parts at least of the Moslem world: with the Moslem martial races of the Indian Empire and with the Arabs whose ways they discovered through Lawrence, Philby and Thesiger. Arab nationalism, Israel and Suez cost Britain the fruits of that empathy, and as Moslem fundamentalism has stolen the clothes of many Moslem moderates, the British have drifted, with other Western countries, into an undifferentiated suspicion of Islam.

Now they see their dealings with the Moslem world through a different prism. Gulf oil weighs heaviest in their calculations, followed by fears of the terrorism that can grow out of religious fundamentalism, frustration in Palestine, or betrayal of Moslem hopes in Bosnia. There is awareness, but little understanding, of the strength of the Moslem faith in Britain itself. The British realise that all these things interact, in a dissatisfied Moslem world that marches with Europe from the southern republics of the former Soviet Union to the Straits of Gibraltar. But they can find no synthesis to pull all these disparate Moslem considerations together.

We come back to Europe. Ten years ago, the Soviet Union was the second most powerful country in the world. For 40 years British soldiers prepared to go out and die when Soviet tanks rolled westwards across the north German plain. We grieved for Ivan Denisovitch and the Czechs of 1968. Now that world is gone, and Russia and the east European countries have a different significance for us. Today, British aid workers talk to you about Bosnia and technical advisers about Latvia in the same way as they talk, in Africa, about Rwanda and Zimbabwe. We are rediscovering eastern Europe and Russia and the Caucasus, but we are far from understanding them. Some see Russia as a Third World problem, others as the world's next economic miracle.

As for the United States, the British like to think that it is the country which they understand best, but they feel about it a disappointment they still hesitate to express. Ever since Pearl Harbor, the United States has been our shield. We saw ourselves as central, with the Americans, to the Atlantic Alliance, overspending decade after decade on military capacity,[12] standing proudly in the gate beside the United States to block the advance of communism. Too often we hedged our European commitments when Washington called. To us the Special Relationship meant something; and it meant something at every level, to the man in the street as much as to the man in Whitehall.

Now it is gradually being borne in upon us that for the Americans it is a love affair of convenience, worth lip service as long as the cold war lasted but politically an embarrassment now because of Britain's loss of power and influence relative to its rivals'. The cry goes up again – and this time it may be true – that America is distancing itself from Europe: it is preoccupied with its domestic needs, with Asia that promises the future, with Latin America on its doorstep. In its dealings with Europe the United States wants a European Union that can speak for the continent and yet which will accommodate itself to American wishes. It sees Russia as its biggest problem in Europe and Germany as its weight-iest partner. Like France, Britain has its value, with its Security Council seat and its useable military capacity, but its place in America's scheme of things is no longer the privileged one we used to think it.

Slowly the British digest these circumstances in the same way that they digest the erratic solipsism of United States foreign policy and the fearful things that emerge from dark corners of the American domestic scene. But still they censor their thoughts about American faults. We half understand that the loss of American intimacy is a consequence of our own decline. We are doubly wounded: by the loss of the lover and by the withering of the attractions that once bound him to us. But there is still more bad news. Confronted with some of the realities of American policy and the problems American society faces at home, we have to face up to the idea of the United States as an inimical, poten-tially even hostile force. That remote possibility will be examined later in this book, when we turn to the Atlantic Alliance and the trans-atlantic relationship. But it needs noting here as the last and perhaps the biggest of Britain's psychological problems as it comes to terms with the outside world.

⌣

The conclusion is that the British today are at sea when they try to es-tablish where they belong in the world. They underestimate their strengths, and paradoxically exaggerate both their weakness and their capacity for independent action. They bring both nervous resentment and an unjustified complacency to their dealings with foreigners. Today, as for over 20 years, these characteristics are being brought par-ticularly to bear on Britain's relationships with its fellow Europeans. But they have their roots deep in geography and history, as well as con-temporary circumstances, and if the focus of Britain's attention shifted tomorrow, to the Commonwealth or to east Asia, for example, the same instincts and emotions would come out of the bag.

Yet there is a more encouraging side to this story. The British have a concern for the outside world to set in contrast with the neglect that characterises so many countries' approach to foreign parts. It is fed by the elements that also feed British edginess about abroad: historical memory and contemporary contacts, together with an uneasy sense of responsibility and even obligation. Part at least of Britain's division over Europe derives from this interest: parliament and public concern themselves with issues that elsewhere among the 15 are taken as technicalities. Rarely will you find in Britain the sublime unconcern for the outside world to be found in the American midwest or in Japan. Germany hawks its international conscience around the world but is slow to emulate Britain's commitment to it. With an engagement of the emotions which they profess to despise, the British still care strongly about the rest of the world.

And there are signs that now they want to bend their minds to deciding where in it they belong. The postwar half century is behind them, the long-drawn-out years of transition from world power to major nation on Europe's flank. However much its shape and their country's place in it continues to exercise the British, European Union membership is a fact. Meanwhile the globe presents other faces, other problems for them to resolve in their bar parlours and letters to the editor. They want to decide how they relate to east Asia, to the Moslem world and the developing countries, to Russia and the United States. Their concern about abroad is a sign of life and engagement, and a reason for hope about their country's future.

1 "We have no eternal allies and we have no perpetual enemies. Our interests are eternal and perpetual, and those interests it is our duty to follow." *Hansard*, 1 March 1848.

2 Thomas Kielinger, *Crossroads and Roundabouts* (Bonn: Bouvier Verlag, 1997).

3 Victor Hugo saw the relationship this way: "There has never been an antipathy between them, only the desire to surpass. France is the adversary of England as better is the enemy of the good". Consider also judgments attributed respectively to Monsignor Ronald Knox and Admiral Lord Nelson: "It takes a Frenchman to commit a mortal sin" and "The only way to talk to a Frenchman is to knock him down".

4 Paul Johnson, *The Offshore Islanders* (London: Phoenix, 1995).

5 On this and innumerable other aspects of European history see Norman Davies, *Europe: A History* (Oxford: Oxford University Press, 1996).

6 Linda Colley, *Britons. Forging the Nation 1707–1837* (London: Pimlico, 1992).

7   Denis Judd, *Empire. The British Imperial Experience from 1765 to the Present* (London: HarperCollins, 1996).

8   James Morris, *Heaven's Command* (London: Faber, 1973).

9   They were as centrally relevant a century later when in 1907 Sir Eyre Crowe wrote in his celebrated memorandum on Britain's relations with France and Germany: "The general character of England's foreign policy is determined by the immutable condition of her geographical situation on the ocean flank of Europe as an island state with vast overseas colonies and dependencies".

10 P J Cain and A G Hopkins, *British Imperialism. Innovation and Expansion, 1688–1914* (London: Longman, 1993).

11 Eric Hobsbawm, *The Age of Empire* (London: Weidenfeld & Nicolson, 1994).

12 Paul Kennedy, *The Rise and Fall of the Great Powers* (New York: Random House, 1987).

4   Assets and instruments

The last two chapters have shown us the British preoccupied with their difficulties. Well-disposed and objective foreigners look rather to their assets, the fashionable among them talking about London's trendiness, the young about the excitements of learning English in Brighton's language schools and the traditionalists about "fair play".

A first characteristic on which many of them focus is the quality of Britain's human capital. Under-educated, blinkered and unimaginative, lacking intellectual rigour, we may be an old, weary and disillusioned nation. But there is here also a basic positive quality, a flexibility of mind and spirit. This may sit oddly with a people notoriously slow to change, instinctively slothful, wedded to tradition, less concerned with the future than with past glories. But make a broad-brush comparison with the peoples of the United States, Germany and Japan; with France and the model societies of Scandinavia; for that matter with the young tigers of east Asia. By many an anecdotal measure, these peoples lack the personal adaptability of so many individual Britons.

Of course national caricatures are no more than that; but the effectiveness of caricature is a function of the reality it reflects and distorts. The caricature Briton is quirky, unpredictable, bad at conceptual thought and long-term planning. The American, by contrast, is a pre-destinarian, committed to the ineluctable fulfilment of manifest destiny, the company's mission, his own career. He is a citizen of a country made great by the certainties of the industrial production line. The German is haunted by the need for the calculable, for predictability and reassurance; the Japanese by his necessary subordination to employer, senior and society. The Frenchman may come closer to the Briton, but in his concern for intellectual consistency, the essence of Gallicism, he too often shies away from empirical common sense. As for the tigers of Asia, some of their ministers confess that their earnest young people are too disciplined and too dutiful, lacking in personal verve and initiative.

Adaptability will be a key strength in tomorrow's world. The realities of post-industrial society require the ability to come to terms with new concepts – of politics and society, of ways of living and earning a living, of a wider world which has suddenly become a part of our domestic lives. The British – perhaps surprisingly – are showing themselves better at the process of adaptation than some of their peers. To the extent that Britain has economically repositioned itself for the better in the last two decades by comparison at least with its European competitors, as most foreign observers believe it has, the credit is partly due to the adaptability of the British character.

A consequence of adaptability is another quality of the British, their tolerance: of strangers, of alternatives, of oddity. It coexists strangely with an equally marked arrogance which has effortlessly outlived national decline. Foreigners invest here, they say, because they find Britain a good place to live and to build their businesses. In today's more mean-spirited society, foreign investors get a readier welcome than refugees or the dispossessed, but Britain's tolerance of difference is deep-rooted: it relishes profound idiosyncrasy, for example. That acceptance makes Britain a more diverse society and a more vibrant one; it also opens it to the risks and rewards of alternative thought and self-expression. Britain is not a nation of immigrants like Canada or Australia, but as a society it accommodates difference more easily than France, Germany and Japan; than the model societies of Scandinavia; and than most parts of the United States. And tolerance makes Britain a more cosmopolitan society, with a cosmopolitanism not just of origin and colour but of style and thought.

⌁

There is more to any country than its capital, but great cities often encapsulate the countries for which they stand. Let us look at London as a principal illustration of the coming together of these qualities of adaptability and tolerance. A Briton can see it as a run-down, embittered place, its qualities submerged in failures.[1] Foreign visitors see something more splendid, perhaps the most complete of world cities. Circumstances have made it currently fashionable among the world's travellers: music, clubs, highly-strung restaurateurs, Andrew Lloyd Webber, the Channel Tunnel, the approbation of American magazines short of a cover story. But London's attractions run wider and deeper than that.

It is the most cosmopolitan city in the world. New Yorkers will dispute that assertion, but New York, for all its rich mix of immigrant and visitor, lacks London's daily influx of visiting continental Europeans. Paris is a proud place, but its grasp does not extend much beyond the European, the Francophone and the Francophile. The building site of today's Berlin may in time turn into a world city, bringing all the rich complexity of central and eastern Europe to the global party, but it will not in two lifetimes achieve the reach beyond Europe that London effortlessly enjoys. There are other places with claims to the cosmopolitan, like San Francisco, Brussels and Singapore, but these are limited, regional metropolises. In London foreigners see the permanence of Westminster and the City, the vigour of Docklands renewal, the "the most rounded city in the world".[2]

London also plays a part in making Britain the world's best connected society, what a new report calls "Britain the global hub",[3] with a range of international contacts surpassing even those of the United States. It owes these connections to many origins. The first is the old British empire, which bound one-quarter of humanity into some sort of relationship with the metropolis. By today's standards its touch was a light one, both in the territories where Britons settled and in those where they ruled over indigenous populations, but it spread an awareness of Britain that has no real historical comparison.[4] By contrast the French empire and the Portuguese, the Dutch settlements and the Belgian, the Russian expansion in central Asia and the Caucasus were all limited affairs, matters essentially of one continent or a few territories.

Many of the connections which the empire built might have been lost at independence, leaving only kith-and-kin links in the old dominions. But the precedent set by India, of republican status within a Commonwealth of which the British sovereign was the personal head, opened the way to the growth of an organisation which now embraces almost all of Britain's former colonies. We shall look at the Commonwealth's structural and operational possibilities in a later chapter. Its relevance here is the institutional umbrella it provides for Britain's myriad contacts with its other members. The informal Commonwealth of non-official organisations and the Commonwealth of people suffer from none of the inhibitions which affect the institution at official and political levels. Its multilateralism enriches the bilateral contacts which Britain has inherited from empire.

But the first British Empire sprang up in the American colonies in the 17th century. These colonies planted the English language and British assumptions which helped shape the United States, so that throughout the 19th century and much of the 20th Britain and the United States were not quite foreign to one another. There is still something about this transatlantic relationship which sets it apart from the United States' relationships with France or Germany: "special" in a sense that has little to do with assertions of Britain's political importance, but rather with personal and institutional understanding. It derives from language, style, method and familiarity.

On the European continent Britain has been adding to its collection of international connections since the Norman conquest. Our European links rival those of France and Italy, although we do not have Germany's depth of contact in eastern and northern Europe. For nearly a quarter of a century now, European Community membership has been adding another dimension of intimacy, a day-in, day-out operational acquaintance between ministers and officials, parliamentarians and lawyers, lobbyists, businessmen and journalists. What is different about these Community relationships is their workaday nature, bringing a kind of collegiate intimacy. Our contacts perhaps fall short of those of other major members of the Community, in part because we came late to it and have so often stood aslant within it, in part because we have never put in the sheer hard work that has built the relationship between Germany and France. But we bring a contribution of our own, in particular our familiarity and contacts with the countries of the Commonwealth and the United States.

Foreign diplomats remark upon a particular skill of British professionals which draws on this range of connections. It is an ability to see the world in the round, to balance one part of it against another, to draw on an asset here to help solve a problem there, and to do so with an exemplary economy of resources and effort. For better or for worse, this skill makes British foreign policy truly global, in a way that is true of none of its partners except the United States and, to a more limited extent, France.

⤺

It is, however, the English language which most foreigners see as Britain's greatest single asset. The figures show that 350 million people speak it as their mother tongue and as many again use it regularly as a second language; and an English expert claims that it is "easily the most adaptable and most varied means of communication ever put together by man – much superior, it should be said, to Latin or even Greek, and far less hampered by rules than either French or German".[5] Whether that opinion is accurate or overblown, English is an essential element in Britain's international connections. Sixty per cent of the world's scientists and 20 per cent of its entire population speak some English. It is an official or semi-official language in 70 countries, and the working language of the official and of much of the informal Commonwealth. If there remains anything "special" about Britain's relationship with the United States, the common language is a major contributory element. In Europe, English is the foreign language of choice almost everywhere. In the worlds of business, science, literature and popular culture, English predominates – more because it is the language of the United States than of Britain, but predominant nevertheless. In time rivals will overtake it, but not in the next quarter century.[6]

Talk of the language of Shakespeare and you give English a historical, almost wistful character. But English is as much an asset for the future as an ornament of the past. It couples more naturally than any of its rivals with the languages of the computer and is the Internet's language of choice. Instantaneous, multimedia communication around the world is most easily accessible from an English-language base. The international information society is as much a matter of numbers and symbols as of letters, of digitalised concepts as of words. But it is the English language which provides the accepted transitions between numbers, symbols and concepts and the material realities for which they stand. All this gives a further dimension to the established reality that global knowledge of English gives British culture, science and communications privileged access to foreign marketplaces. And if the technological media follows the language, the message follows the media.

~

There can be no doubt that Britain's reputation overseas changed with its decline in political and economic weight in the world in the late 1940s. The empire went the way of Nineveh and Tyre, and the Commonwealth, valuable as it is, tells a less certain, if often more af-fectionate, story about Britain than the empire once did. The United States now looks to a single Europe as well as a variety of European powers, where once it looked essentially to Britain. We have seemed wilfully determined not to build a positive reputation on the European continent, and although the situation is not hopeless, it will take con-sistent hard work to rebuild our position there. To east Asia we are a diminished place, of interest essentially as a significant member of a European whole.

Yet across a broad front the reputation of Britain and the British remains robust. Much of that reputation depends on the strengths of our institutions. Transient folly apart, Westminster-style government retains international resonance. So do the rigour of our administrative system and the forcefulness of our centralised system of government. The Diplomatic Service, the British Council, the World Service and above all the armed forces enjoy a high reputation abroad. Japan envies us our global reach and knowledge. German industrialists would like to emulate some of the flexibility of British business. Despite the shadow cast by our hesitations on the European single currency, the salience of British financial services is rising, not falling. The professions set world standards in fields as different as accountancy, medicine and engineering. Britain has a strong reputation in literature and theatre, and a fluctuating but always prominent place in the fickle world of popular and youth culture. In foreign eyes Britain remains a good place to do business, with politicians, government, industry, the City, the media and academia. It is not the pre-eminent place of yesteryear; nor is it the ineffectual, well-nigh hopeless place of much British caricature.

For 40 years after the Second World War, British manufacturing industry lost ground in world markets. Its inadequacies lay at the heart of the country's failure relative to its competitors, and did more than anything else to diminish Britain's reputation in the eyes of foreign observers. But in the last ten years it has reformed itself, improved its performance, and stabilised and even marginally improved its competitive position. It is now the fifth most substantial international trader, its position threatened but not yet overtaken by the new young giants of Asia. There are great differences between the stronger sectors and the weaker, between the performance of individual companies, and between UK Ltd's performance in different parts of the globe.[7] But Britain's companies taken together have just under 4 per cent of the United States market, 3 per cent of Japan's, and 6–10 per cent of the markets of the main European countries. Britain has the second largest pool of overseas investment, much of it in manufacturing; and the inward direct investment which it has attracted has played a large part in the improvement of its industrial performance of the last decade. Overall, manufacturing industry gives Britain a solid position in the world economy, and its performance no longer occasions the pity or contempt of foreigners..

Financial services are by most measures more successful and hold more promise in a post-industrial world. The cities of London, Edinburgh and Leeds contribute to making Britain the second biggest exporter of financial services in the world and they hold a more commanding lead over new rivals than do most sectors of British industry. London, in particular, is attractive to foreign competitors, who buy up its investment banking houses and base their operations there. As the developed world becomes increasingly dependent on services for its livelihood, this great comparative advantage should be increasingly valuable to UK Ltd as a whole.

But the sector remains controversial. Traditionally, controversy focused on the City's impact on manufactures. The charge was that banking had failed to give manufacturing industry the sustained support that it enjoys in Germany; that to maintain its international position the City had demanded of government financial and fiscal policies that restricted economic growth; that Britain's investment managers funnelled abroad capital that might have gone into manufacturing; and that the relationship between the country's financial and political classes amounted to an unholy alliance against industry and industrial employment.[8]

Elements of that controversy linger today, but it has largely been overtaken by a new one. This centres on the interplay between Britain's financial industries and European Union, and particularly single currency membership. The City has been convinced for more than 20 years of the intellectual merits of European Community membership and of a successful single currency, and accepts its implications for closer union. But it also sees the economic dangers of a failure of economic and monetary union, the political danger that Britain will exclude itself from it, the threat to its own position from centres such as Frankfurt operating from within the single currency, and the need to keep its own options open as a centre for the world's financial needs. Hence a lingering ambiguity about its position on this most sensitive of issues as the evidence piles up that in 1999 the enterprise will go ahead on time, if without Britain.

∽

Britain's intellectual and cultural assets are less sensitive to the winds of politics and economics, and make a major contribution to its international position and reputation. Its universities and scientific resources attract foreign respect: not the unqualified regard they once enjoyed, nor the respect accorded to the United States' strongest institutions, but an esteem which makes them national properties of value. So do individual British scholars, and in particular British specialists in other civilisations. Literature, popular music, the arts and the theatre makes similar contributions. Comparisons are crude as well as odious; but it is difficult to see Italy, for example, overtaking Britain's intellectual and cultural position in the world as by some measures it has overtaken the

British economy. And the British Council makes effective use of these assets in its cultural diplomacy and representation.

Britain is similarly disproportionately strong in international communications. The World Service of the BBC attracts perhaps more than its share of attention here; but it is a substantial national asset. So are the BBC's more general exports, and those of ITV and Reuters. In one sense, successful international communications do not merely reach beyond frontiers but render them irrelevant. In another, British-based international communications help spread British scholarship, culture, entertainment, political opinions and values to the world. They can involve the country in controversy, as when BBC broadcasts offend authoritarian regimes or when the output of Rupert Murdoch's British-based media conflicts with his global ambitions; but that does not diminish their positive value. Yet like the British Council, the BBC World Service and other broadcasters are ill-served by the uncritical adulation which many foreigners, quite as much as Britons, heap upon them.

Both the British Council and the World Service make calls upon the taxpayer, but by comparison with them Britain's official overseas development programme is a major spender. The Department for International Development, newly independent from the Foreign and Commonwealth Office, spends £2.2 billion a year on the world's sixth largest national aid programme, roughly commensurate to Britain's position as its fifth largest international trader. Trade may provide the most prominent element in Britain's overseas links but aid connects it to the desperately poor. It promotes development out of poverty, encourages good government and accountability, tackles human and natural catastrophes, contributes to international stability and builds markets for British exports. Whether it does these things effectively, and on a sufficient scale, or whether charity should instead begin at home is the stuff of undying political controversy. The case for overseas aid is the stronger if you accept the Labour government's emphasis on ethical considerations among Britain's overseas concerns. Whatever the individual judgment, Britain's international development programme forms a significant part of the nation's overseas profile, and in particular of its influence in the developing world.

Intelligence, by contrast, still operates in the shadows. In the last decade Britain's intelligence institutions have tried to dispense with unnecessary mystification and the years in which British diplomats professed to know nothing of intelligence are done. But it remains of necessity a secretive trade. For years secrecy about British intelligence, combined with its wartime and postwar achievements, brought it intrigued respect. Foreigners paid their own tribute to it, sometimes in the conviction that British intelligence knew everything. It is the principal field in which Britain retains a true special relationship with the United States.

Now there are arguments for a refocused intelligence effort. Information has replaced steel or coal as the sinews of national power. Significant parts of that information are secret. We need a capacity to extract them from the airwaves, chanceries, armed forces and terrorist cells of the world. With the Soviet target gone, we are told, British intelligence is turning its attention to new targets: terrorists, drug runners, international crime, money launderers, all of them legitimate targets, for they have a real capacity to damage ordinary Britons. Yet Britain's intelligence machine appears to cost in total about £1 billion a year and to employ about 10,000 people.[9] Expenditure is declining, but it will remain in the next century a major charge on the public purse. It prompts urgent questions about value for money and the need for an effort on such a scale. The nature of the intelligence business is such that the outsider cannot hope to judge needs, methods and effectiveness. In a sense, we still take intelligence on trust, and that leaves us uneasy. But without adequate intelligence, we might find ourselves taking an unpredictable and competitive world on trust. I prefer to trust our own intelligence panjandrums, suitably constrained by administrative and parliamentary oversights, rather than potential enemies.

Part of our intelligence effort trades under diplomatic cover, and intelligence operatives make up a part of Britain's diplomatic apparatus. But whatever Le Carré and the old Soviet analogy may suggest to the contrary, the Diplomatic Service is much more than a cover for Britain's licensed snoopers. It represents Britain to foreign governments. It interprets the doings and potential of other states to British ministers. It conducts Britain's international negotiations. It promotes British commerce. It protects the British citizen abroad. It concerns itself with visas, passports and the government's overseas publicity. To a business consultant it is a dangerously unfocused conglomerate. To its competitors it is the best diplomatic machine in the world.

Yet like the British Council, the World Service and British intelligence, the Diplomatic Service consumes taxpayers' money. Its operating costs are over £500 million a year. Add £94 million in subscriptions to the United Nations and other organisations, £70 million for military training and other services to the developing world, £20 million for peacekeeping, the £2.2 billion cost of Britain's official overseas development assistance programme and the bills for the British Council and the BBC World Service, and Britain is spending more than £3 billion of public money a year on its international business.[10]

This is serious money: the Diplomatic Service's operating costs alone would keep ten general hospitals in operation, and the grand total of the country's expenditure on diplomacy, intelligence and aid amounts to 16 per cent of the Ministry of Defence's budget. We cannot dismiss it, as the Diplomatic Service's apologists sometimes seek to do, as peanuts. But Britain maintains diplomatic relations with more than 180 countries. To conduct them, and to provide a global service to the businessman and the traveller abroad, Britain maintains 218 posts overseas. It is an effort roughly comparable to that of other internationally active countries of our size.

How cost-effectively does the Diplomatic Service conduct its business? It is painfully, even plaintively, conscious of the economies it has made over the years. That it has done so, and remains the effective machine it is, is a tribute to its rigour; or, if you take a more sceptical view, evidence of the fat it carried and an indication that it may have more to give up. All this is not a subject that lends itself to decisive outside judgment or even to generalisation; but that will not prevent interested observers attempting both. Let me offer mine, reinforced by what I believe to be the honest opinions of foreign observers.

It is the effectiveness of the Diplomatic Service rather than its marginal cost which is most relevant to a survey of Britain's assets, and of that there is little informed doubt. For better or worse, it punches above the nation's weight. Its missions in Brussels, New York and

Washington, the diplomatically most competitive cities in the world, are regularly highly rated by demanding critics. So are its staffs in lesser places. It speaks a bewildering variety of difficult languages. It delivers high-quality service to ministers. It gives good value for money.

But with its effectiveness come costs, over and above the money costs which so preoccupy attention. The first is the diversion of high-quality manpower from other, conceivably more useful tasks. Here the Diplomatic Service may form part of a phenomenon that has often been blamed for Britain's relative failure: the alleged distaste of educated Britons for wealth creation, for the market, for the real world, and their preference instead for the professions, academia and public service. Twenty years ago this was the stuff of reports to governments. Whether it is cogent still, whether it ever represented observable reality, is a moot point, but it remains an issue worth noting if not, in this context, detailed examination.

The second cost of a high-powered Diplomatic Service is the danger that it will command too much of the nation's attention or resources for foreign affairs. Perhaps Britain should beware of buying influence at the price of more concrete interests. Certainly there is a possibility that active and sensitive officials will come to understand too well the preoccupations of the foreigners with whom they deal, and give them disproportionate weight. They need the counterweight of the endlessly repeated question, "Where do Britain's interests lie?". But that question in turn has no simple or short-term answers. If we seek Britain's all-round interests, as we should, we are looking for one thread in a closely woven tapestry; and if we want to do them justice we must look not just to this week's triumph but to the country's positioning into the next century.

For those, like me, who ate the salt of the Diplomatic Service for decades, it is difficult to be entirely objective about all this. For a more dispassionate British opinion look to "True Brits".[11] But wherever exactly you strike the balance, few objective foreign observers would see the Diplomatic Service as less than a valuable instrument in tackling Britain's overseas agenda.

As instruments of value in Britain's work overseas, the armed forces are in a sense the Diplomatic Service, the aid programme, the British Council, the World Service and the intelligence services in spades. Their professionalism is comparable. Their reputation abroad is as great, and their popularity at home much greater. Their cost, like their potential capacity, is very much greater. They lack the intrinsic versatility of the civilian services, yet by the standards of most armed forces they are highly adaptable to a broad range of post-cold war roles. Guns remain the last argument of foreign policy.

Britain's armed forces cost more than £20 billion a year. They provide a submarine-borne nuclear deterrent; a major land, sea and air contribution to NATO; a contribution to security in Northern Ireland; a limited capacity to project power worldwide; a highly effective national contribution to United Nations peacekeeping operations; and the ability to provide training to friendly countries in the developing world and in eastern Europe. They are the country's ultimate protection, and a major national asset.

They are also, some argue, a distraction from other priorities. Britain has cut its defence spending to 2.7 per cent of its GDP on defence, still well above the NATO average of 2.3 per cent. It is almost universally acknowledged that what the armed forces do they do well. But there is also a widely held conviction that in the post-cold war world not all their work is necessary; that they could be smaller and less expensive; that some part of that £20 billion should be channelled into a "peace dividend"; and that the very excellence of Britain's armed forces constitutes a standing temptation to take on more tasks abroad than the country's interests demand.

Even in the cold war, the nuclear deterrent aroused very divided reactions. To some it was Britain's ticket to the international top table; an ultimate assurance against Soviet attack and American defection; and a vital element of strength to put in the balance beside French nuclear capacity on the European scene. To others it was expensive, in terms both of money and self-delusion; ultimately incredible; an obstacle to the campaign against nuclear proliferation; and morally unacceptable. Now, in its critics' eyes, it has been stripped of its last justification. There is, they contend, no conceivable target; this is an argument which leaves its supporters pointing to remaining Russian nuclear capacity, to weapons of mass destruction in the hands of rogue states and individuals, and to Europe's need in an uncertain world for a nuclear capacity of its own.

Meanwhile, Britain's need to be able to fight a war in Europe has been reduced, and has perhaps vanished, with the collapse of the Soviet Union and the Warsaw Pact. Its armoured forces and air strike capacity in Germany have been reduced in consequence. And while these changes have been taking place, the need for a capacity to fight brush fires and keep the peace has grown.

Now British forces are deployed from the Gulf to the Falklands. They mostly play a useful stabilising role: containing trouble, relieving hardship, holding the ring while diplomacy goes to work. They are adept at winning hearts and minds. In most instances they are deployed in cooperation with the forces of other nations, demonstrating that in today's world good company brings reassurance and respectability. If all goes well, the end result is the defence of the reasonably good or the less bad against the worse. To many, this is the acceptable face of soldiering, and our skills at it bring unquestionable benefit to Britain.

Against this, we should remember that in the 1960s and 1970s military bases worldwide, at first incontestably assets, were slowly transmogrified into liabilities: consider the Suez base, or Singapore, or perhaps now the sovereign base areas in Cyprus. There is a similar danger with deployments in support of international good causes today, the more acute if the object of an intervention, or the feasibility of its operation, is uncertain. Such interventions can go horribly wrong, for foreign troops as much as failed and failing states themselves. This is what happened to United States and French forces in Lebanon, to United States and Italian forces in Somalia; and, in vastly more terrible circumstances, to the whole United States intervention in Vietnam. Such considerations will not always outweigh a manifest political and humanitarian need to do something to assuage the agony of states that fail. They do not diminish the credit of the armed forces' performance in many trouble spots. But they do sound a note of warning to be heeded when the television cameras bring us the message that "something must be done".[12]

There is a broader danger that flows from the professionalism of Britain's armed forces. For a country that believes it is in some ways doing badly, there is a temptation to give undue prominence to what it does well. Britain has faced that danger for two generations, all the way from the endless re-fighting of the Second World War to the exaltation of the SAS and the pride of the Falklands campaign and Desert Storm. We have much to be proud of. Throughout the cold war we were proud to be western Europe's most resolute military nation. The inclination is there still. Our problem in deciding how to deploy our military resources around the world is to exploit their value while keeping in proportion what we spend on them and what we do with them.

1   Patrick Wright, *A Journey through Ruins: The Last Days of London* (London: Radius, 1990).

2   German businessman discussing direct investment in Britain in conversation with the author, 1983.

3   Mark Leonard, *The Independent*, 8 September 1997, introducing his book, *Britain, Renewing our Identity* (London: Demos, 1997).

4   The best popular description of the strengths and weaknesses of the empire remains James Morris's trilogy, *Heaven's Command, Pax Britannica* and *Farewell the Trumpets* (London: Faber, 1973, 1968 and 1978 respectively).

5   Geoffrey Elton, *The English* (Oxford: Blackwell, 1992).

6   For evidence of the gradual and surprising decline of the English language's global pre-eminence see Samuel P Huntington, *The Clash of Civilizations and the Remaking of World Order* (New York: Simon & Schuster, 1996).

7   Michael E Porter, *The Competitive Advantage of Nations* (London: Macmillan, 1990).

8   For a detailed survey of the argument see P J Cain and A G Hopkins, *British Imperialism Crisis and Deconstruction, 1914–1990* (London: Longman, 1993).

9   Michael Herman, *Intelligence Power in Peace and War* (Cambridge: Cambridge University Press, 1996).

10 *Foreign and Commonwealth Office 1997 Departmental Report* (London: Her Majesty's Stationery Office, 1997).

11 Ruth Dudley Edwards, *True Brits: Inside the Foreign Office* (London: BBC Books, 1994).

12 Jane O M Sharp (ed.) *About Turn, Forward March with Europe. New Directions for Defence and Security Policy* (London: Rivers Oram Press, 1996).

5 The flawed colossus

Any exploration of Britain's place in the world has to include an early visit to the United States. This is the globe's most important country, as much because of its intellectual as its economic or military power. It is committed to important principles: the will of the people, accountable government, the rule of law. American minds are active in articulating and developing the concepts of a good society. Government, private organisations and individuals promote them abroad. The power of the United States is an essential element in the alliances and international relationships which bring some uneasy stability to the world. American technology and industry widen mankind's material horizons. The United States' capacity to reshape the affairs of the rest of humanity far exceeds that of any other international actor. So does its will to do so: isolationism may come and go, but Americans have an inherited conviction that the rest of the world would be a better place if it became more like the United States, and some persistent willingness to help it make the change.

America has a special meaning for Britain. Although there is no country that is not to some degree mesmerised by America, Britain has particular reasons for its fascination. The United States was born out of Britain's rib. The two countries began by fighting sanguinary wars against one another, but throughout the 19th century neither treated the other as entirely foreign. The 20th brought two world wars and a cold war fought side by side, and a habit of partnership spiced by recurring irritations. They speak the same language: London's summer streets are peopled by tourists from California telling cockneys that they do, all evidence to the contrary notwithstanding.

The politics of each country has a resonance for the other, and the good opinion of an American president has greater public value to a British prime minister than that of any of the European heads of government with whom he has so much more daily business. The business and intellectual lives of the two countries interpenetrate one another, with a greater equality than the differences in their sizes would lead one to expect. British businessmen chair American banks and American professors enrich British universities. There is a real interest in the other's doings, which outweighs equally real suspicions and dislikes. The British are more than willing to go along with the idea of American exceptionalism. For many Americans there is something special about Britain.[1] For Britain the United States is, in the words my mother used too often of my father, impossible to live with but impossible to live without.

⤸

There is no need here to recount the story of America's rise to greatness.[2] In retrospect we can see how clearly it was pre-ordained. Put together hungry and energetic immigrants with a continent's worth of space and untouched raw materials. Set this paradise two oceans' safe remove from older worlds. Give it – Mexican, Indian and Spanish wars and one terrible civil war excepted – a century of peace and uninterrupted growth. The result was the emergence by 1900 of a nation potentially the richest and most powerful in the world. Involve it, belatedly, fresh and powerful, in two world wars, and the United States emerged as a predominant force. Set it for half a century against the only other continental superpower, while it gathered allies and clients about it. Factor in the Soviet Union's collapse and you are left with a United States unchallengeable in many fields and prominent among the leaders in all the others.

That is the position today's America has inherited. It is the world's only fully grown colossus. It has space: with the continental United States alone sprawling across four time zones and with more than 9 million square kilometres in all, it is the fourth largest country in the world. It ranks seventh in terms of natural resources per head of population.[3] It has more people than any country except China and India, with a spread of education and skills that is the envy of the rest of the world. It is manifestly supreme militarily, spending on national security as much as the next five military powers combined. Economically, America's supremacy is challenged and may not survive very far into the next century, but in 1998 its economy remains almost half as big again as Japan's; and having lost ground to Asian competitors, it has shown in the last decade remarkable powers of industrial recuperation.

But American capacity reaches beyond the conventional measures of economic and military strength. It is still, beyond any other, the land of innovation. Its industries and services deliver freshly conceived and precisely targeted satisfactions to the consumer. Its management skills are a match for Asian challengers. American academics and thinkers provide intellectual muscle, and a willingness to use it about the nation's business. Microsoft and Intel dominate the world's information technology. Americans shape the world's popular culture. Of all the world's major nations, the United States is at every level from the Nobel Prize winner to the man in the street the most articulate.

Yet America today also faces many of the problems which afflict most mature industrial societies. Fifty unbroken years of economic success have aroused expectations that are increasingly difficult to satisfy. The son is no longer automatically better off than his father. The old ethical and moral norms no longer command automatic respect; and while religion plays a bigger part than in any other industrialised society, exaggeration and fundamentalism bring social strains. So does the nation's very size. And the United States is finding it as difficult as others to adapt to the political changes brought by the end of the cold war.

To many observers, therefore, the United States, despite its manifold blessings, seems the most deeply troubled of all the advanced societies. It is arguable that it is American individualism that so dramatically brings out the worst as well as the best in its society.[4] It may look so troubled because it has advanced further into the woes of a changing world than other societies which follow in its footsteps. America's failings do not yet call in question its political, economic and intellectual power, nor its global pre-eminence, but they do threaten its own self-confidence and others' trust in it.

Central to the United States' 19th-century achievement was its success as a melting pot, creating good Americans out of disparate material. But today ethnicity is reasserting itself, making the country a deeply divided place, populated by hyphenated Americans. "American values" and "American boys" remain the stuff of political rhetoric; but individual Americans increasingly identify themselves by colour or origin, or by a set of social and economic interests that in a less sanctimonious society would be labelled "class". With division goes extremism: an extravagance of emotion, thought, expression and action. It is exemplified by the passion that goes into condemning enemies, whether they be the president himself, a demonised United Nations, abortionists or the religious right. Such exaggeration has deep roots in American life, but it is aggravated now by the obsessions of single-issue interest groups and the totalitarianism of political correctness.

All these things reflect and feed on a nation's underlying mood. We have seen that Britain looks back on half a century of relative decline, while the United States has behind it half a century of achievement and fulfilment, building prosperity at home and victory in the cold war abroad. Yet it feels itself cheated of the fruits of those successes. Faced like Britons with accelerating economic change, Americans feel uncertainty about what lies ahead. For in the United States even more than other industrial societies, economic change is dividing society. The demands of technological change and the information economy underline the differing economic worth of those who can contribute and those who cannot, sending them down diverging paths in life. No industrialised society is immune from this tendency to division but the United States is further down the road to national fragmentation than its competitors.[5]

The victims of change fight back against dispossession. Ordinary people deprived of their sense of security turn to populist solutions, scapegoating imports, the export of jobs, free trade, the crimes and sloth of the underclass with its demand on their hard paid taxes. The gated suburbs into which they withdraw are as much mental as physical, setting up barriers to empathy with people whose situation differs from their own. Ordinary poor Americans, particularly the ageing male of traditional industrial America, find that their contribution to the economy goes on declining in value and with it their own well-being and status in society. They seek to distinguish themselves from the un-employed, unmotivated underclass who populate the worst corners of America's cities. The position of both groups is bad, but that of the un-derclass is exacerbated by racial tensions, by drug trafficking and abuse, and by a decline in social self-discipline even more marked than in Britain. At the same time the American possessing classes are less in-hibited than the British in drawing conclusions about the shortcomings of the people at the bottom of the pile. The result is yet more polaris-ation, the abandonment of the inner cities as beyond redemption, the block condemnation of young black males, bloated prison populations and the horrors of death row.

This may sound like a litany of malevolent anti-Americanism, but for America's friends and clients the points it illustrates are important ones. The richest and most successful nation in the world cannot claim to offer all its citizens the blessings of a good society. Perhaps no nation in the world can. But the United States' shortcomings matter more than those of European societies, or of Japan and China. For Ameri-cans' sense of their mission in the world has always been driven by be-lief in that exceptionalism. They are today more triumphalist than ever, yet with a declining faith in themselves. The United States still has more pulling power than any other country, but it no longer provides a model for the world, no longer offers the "last, best hope of mankind". And we cannot exclude the possibility that the dark forces in American life could make it not the basically reliable if often unpre-dictable friend we are used to but an antipathetic and even malign in-fluence upon the world.[6]

～

The domestic flaws of the American colossus have an immense signif-icance for the rest of the world, for they sap its willingness to get in-volved in problems beyond its borders, and its authority there. Yet both willingness and authority are as vitally important as ever. Without them, the alliances which the United States sustains in Europe, Asia and Latin America would fall apart. The American commitment to world order is already shaky, as its United Nations payments record il-lustrates; but its interventions – arbitrary and belated as they may be –

are indispensable to the solution of the problems of failed states. Without the United States' ubiquitous involvement, as market, exporter, investor, innovator and guarantor of the dollar, the world trading system would be set back decades. For all these reasons governments and businesses everywhere hang day by day upon the words of Washington and New York.[7]

Those words have always been uncertain ones, for Americans have always had a divided heart about the rest of the world. They have a natural difficulty in taking foreigners entirely seriously. To a successful nation of immigrants they must always seem failed Americans, the people who lacked the get-up-and-go to make their way to the emigrant ships and the land of the free. New Americans still come to the United States to escape from less satisfactory societies, refreshing strong isolationist instincts. But they also, like their predecessors, bring connections with the lands from which they come. The consequence is that tensions between isolationist tendencies and interventionist instincts persist more than 50 years after Franklin Roosevelt seemed to have routed them for good.[8]

Throughout the half century or so since Pearl Harbor, the world has grown accustomed to America being involved in all its doings. To America it owes the destruction of two totalitarian systems, the creation and sustenance of a network of alliances that between them have done more good than harm, the maintenance of a rough and ready stability within which much of the world has grown out of poverty, and a critically important and dynamic contribution to the world economy. To crown all this came the collapse of the Soviet Union, the fall of communism and victory in the cold war: if not the end of history at least the close of a glorious chapter in it. It did not seem unreasonable for George Bush to talk at the beginning of the 1990s of a New World Order, sustained by United States power and enriched by American principles.

Reality has proved more uncertain, as Americans dedicated to very different priorities have once again had their say. With the Soviet threat removed and Saddam Hussein's armies destroyed, no powerful enemy has threatened American interests. Iran, Iraq, Libya, North Korea, Cuba, terrorists and drug-runners, all these in their different ways challenged the United States, but none required the full deployment of

America's imperial might. It was the problems of an unself-confident and self-pitying society at home that demanded attention: "The economy, stupid", as in Bill Clinton's reiterated campaign reminder, was the priority; and with it, health care, inner cities, a fragmenting nation. By contrast John F Kennedy's assertion that "we shall pay any price, bear any burden, meet any hardship, support any friend, oppose any foe"[9] has little resonance in modern America.

Americans who argued for domestic priorities in the early 1990s could point to the fact that the outside world was a different place. The Europeans, so long fragmented, were building what looked like the beginnings of a United States of Europe. The Atlantic world was no longer under threat. But in the Pacific, Japan's economy seemed to threaten America's. The experience of defending the New World Order proved ungrateful in Somalia and Haiti. The United States could not contract out of the world's affairs, but its involvement with them would have to be careful, considered, limited and practical.

Yet for a country with America's global interests, even partial disengagement was a chimera. All the things that had made the United States a superpower made escape from responsibility impossible. Just like Gulliver, America was still held captive by a thousand threads, each of them flimsy but together unbreakable. Thus America's diverse instincts about abroad – isolationism, benevolent imperialism and the pursuit of its material interests – were forced back into uneasy coalition.[10]

The result is a continued but grudging commitment to the world's business. American policy is less spasmodic than it was, but still hesitant and uncertain. American leaders and officials see the world in all its complexity, but their policies are shaped by the need to justify them to an electorate which is wary of abroad, wedded to sound-bite policy-making and preoccupied with events at home. Only major direct threat to American interests seems likely to alter this. A resurgent Russia might yet pose such a threat, as might an assertive China. But far more obvious threats to what ordinary Americans see as their interests come from trade competitors, from terrorists and drug dealers, and from the threat to their jobs posed by their country's commitment to a free world trading system. The world is not going to see a consistently assertive United States. The problem for its friends, therefore, is to engage its interest in foreign problems, secure its commitment where its involvement is essential and dissuade it from actions driven by domestic circumstances which can do such disproportionate damage beyond its borders.

∽

Britain has a particular interest in ensuring that America remains engaged with the problems of the globe. It stands at the junction of the Atlantic and European worlds. As a permanent member of the Security Council and one of the world's leading peace-keepers it sees the need for a better relationship between the United States and the United Nations, and for American company and strength in the world's trouble spots. It is even more dependent than most of its peers on the smooth functioning of the world economy, still largely shaped by American policies. And rightly or wrongly it thinks of itself as America's particular friend. Ever since the Battle of Britain in 1940, a mainspring of British foreign policy has been this concern to get America involved on Britain's side and to keep it involved as a partner in European and world affairs. It was that concern which drove Britain's year-in-year-out loyalty to the United States throughout the cold war. The reasons for it remain valid today.[11]

The American commitment which still matters most to Britain is its leadership of the Atlantic Alliance. The traditional Soviet threat is gone, with Russian troops pulled back all the way to the gates of St Petersburg. But Europe still faces security problems. In the short term, Russian weakness throws up challenges which only Europe working together with America can contain; in the longer term the threat posed by a Russia reborn could require all the resources of a superpower to contain it. Eastern Europe, and the Balkans in particular, are dangerously unstable, and Bosnia has shown us the indispensability of American strength when events spin out of control. And the NATO countries are faced by a new order of challenges, from terrorism, organised crime, illegal immigration and rogue states, all of which point the need for continuing transatlantic cooperation.[12]

Britain also seeks a more consistent American commitment to the United Nations and to world order. The record on both illustrates both the indispensability of the United States and the extent to which its attitudes to the outside world are driven by the vagaries of domestic politics. There can, for example, be no defence of the United States' continuing default on its financial obligations to the United Nations, nor of its determination unilaterally to reduce them; yet a continuing United Nations is unimaginable without American membership. Similarly the story of American involvement in overseas interventions and peacekeeping operations, whether organised by the United Nations or otherwise, runs erratically from many Caribbean excursions over the years through Somalia in 1992 to Bosnia today; yet, as Bosnia has shown, action without the United States lacks conviction and effectiveness. Many parts of the developing world will succumb to crises which demand outside intervention. So in the field of world order as much as that of European security, Britain has a major interest in securing a prompt American commitment to action and in ensuring that it is not prematurely broken off.

American political and economic interests around the Pacific face British policy makers with a different range of problems. They want to help ensure that the United States does not so far succumb to the attractions of east Asia as to lose interest in Europe. At the same time, they know that only the United States can provide the additional political and military muscle that will be needed if existing tensions in east Asia, and particularly between China and its neighbours, run out of control. Britain and Europe also want their share of the benefits of the growing east Asian and Pacific Rim economies. So in looking to the Pacific, so remote and yet potentially so important to our economic interests, Britain will have to do what it can with its European partners to ensure that the coming "Pacific century" falls victim neither to collision nor collusion between Asia and the United States.

Britain has, finally, an interest in doing what little it can to ensure that American attention is not distracted from Europe by other issues. The most salient is Latin America, where United States' domestic and international concerns clearly intersect. Latin America faces the United States with great economic opportunities – Mexico alone is, for example, its third biggest export market, almost twice the size of the United Kingdom – and with perennial political and security problems. From Latin America come the drugs that fuel gang wars in North America's inner cities. And from the Caribbean and across the Rio Grande comes a steady flow of immigrants, legal and illegal, who are helping change the balance of United States society.

All these issues – Atlantic security, the United Nations and world order, the new forces emerging in east Asia and other distractions of American attention – place demands on the relationship between the United States and western Europe which has lain for half a century at the heart of the democratic world. It is a relationship which extends beyond the Atlantic Alliance and NATO into wider fields, and engages with the questions about the future of Europe and the European Union which form the subject of the next two chapters. When Europe and the United States look at one another they are concerned with characteristics, qualities and defects that go far wider than the political and economic stuff of formal international relations. So the history, culture and sociology which have helped shape these two very different societies, which pull British hearts and minds in different directions, are worth exploring here.

The United States can claim, reasonably correctly, that it has had a consistent policy towards Europe and European integration for more than 40 years. It wants a strong and united partner on the other side of the Atlantic, Kennedy's single second pillar of the Alliance, the single European voice that successive American presidents have always said they wanted to hear and would attend to. Today, when Americans complain about Europe, their grievance is more often about European disunity and ineffectuality than the tendency to caucus before engaging in transatlantic dialogue. Of course, when Europe does speak as one, as in trade disputes, spokesmen for sectional American interests whistle a different tune, but there is no reason to believe that the United States would be strategically unhappy if it were faced, one fine day, with a United States of Europe across the ocean. It is worth asking how it would cope with that or with a Europe achieving a lesser degree of integration.

Western Europe and America have much in common. They have largely grown from common European, Hebraic and Christian roots. They account together for over 600 million people, dedicated to good things they value in common, like personal freedom, accountable government, the rule of law, and peace and prosperity for all. They share the 20th century's great success story, having successfully resisted together a different system of values and made Europe whole.

They face the same challenges, from the possibility of a resurgent Russia through Moslem fundamentalism to the competition of the Asian industrial states.

But Europe and the United States are very different places. America's films and literature tell us that it is the most individualist of all the great societies, and has been since its origins. The ideas of freedom and of individual responsibility are central to the American psyche: the individual is free to rise and free to fall, owing little to and expecting little of society or the state. They lie at the root of the United States' strengths and weaknesses.

The European instinct is very different. An inheritance that goes back to the mediaeval authority of church and feudal superior means that Europeans know their place. The 17th and 18th centuries gave them strong, centralised states. While 19th-century Americans were growing free, their European cousins were still bound to deference. When they rebelled they sought not individual freedom but socialism and the protection it gave to all. A majority of today's Europeans still opts for the social market economy, for society, for the well-being of the group, for gentler if less efficient ways. In all this, many continental Europeans in particular are the Americans' polar opposites. When Europeans and Americans work together effectively, as they so often do, it is a complementary relationship, not a matching of like with like.

It is also the world's most important relationship. The continuing rise of the countries of east Asia will complicate it and distract both parties. But nothing is going to reduce either the United States or Europe to ineffectuality. They have too, together with Canada and the Antipodes, many of the qualities an often distraught world requires. They have, for example, a kind of moral seriousness and sense of responsibility that it is hard to find replicated elsewhere. This is illustrated by their commitment, patchy as it may be, to their peacekeeping role under the United Nations, and by their efforts to find a balance in their domestic affairs between the individual's rights, the good of the community and the interests of efficiency, an approach that is quite different from that of east Asia.

The two parts of the Atlantic world share also a certain kind of intellectual vigour and inventiveness; they may fear Asia's competition, but America and Europe are not intellectual or technological down-

and-outs. They have political muscle, both domestic and foreign; the capacity to mobilise society behind government in great causes and to put their muscle to work in the world's negotiating chambers. These qualities cannot be as readily identified elsewhere on the globe. They make the strategic differences between Europe and America less important than their similarities.

⌒

Britain stands at the meeting point between these two different but complementary Atlantic societies. In its domestic concerns, the preference for the continental or the American model underlies many differences of political and economic opinion. In international affairs it has bent its best efforts since the Second World War to binding Europe and America together. It believes that it understands continental Europe better than America can, and it still professes to interpret the United States to Europe. We shall see in the next two chapters how far Britain has to go before it is truly at ease with its continental neighbours. But it shares the European understanding of limited possibilities as no American can, and it is built on the same scale as its European neighbours. Operationally it is locked into day-to-day Brussels business as the United States is not. As for interpreting America to Europe, every European country and the European Commission itself have their own range of contacts, experiences and interests. But history, language and everyday familiarity make Britain's range richer than those of its partners. It is one of the assets it brings to the European Union.[13]

So Britain sees itself destined to interpret between the Atlantic and the continent, between Europe and the United States. The right way to do so is as a committed European power vividly aware of the importance of the Atlantic relationship and determined to ensure that our neighbours see it as complementary to the European vocation. But Britain's persisting doubts about its place in Europe remain a fact. There are still Britons seeking alternatives to open-ended commitment to a Europe moving towards "ever closer union".

The world, they argue, is a big place, and a rapidly changing one. The dynamism of east Asia is manifest, as is the promise of much of the developing world. The United States is the only superpower, and a friendly one. It is folly to coop ourselves up in a Europe which is still pursuing an integrationist, collectivist nostrum that may have made sense in the 1960s and 1970s but which is sadly outdated today. Britain belongs where it always has, on the high seas of the world. But it has long since lost the political and military capacity to go it alone. It should therefore bind itself to its American cousin, with which it has not just history and language in common but a modern social philosophy and an economic style quite different from the Europeans'.

For those convinced that the European Union means only trouble for Britain, it is a seductive argument, and one to which we return at various points in this book. But this is the place to examine the feasibility and desirability of the idea of recreating a special link to the United States, to be enjoyed by Britain alone or by Britain in common with other, perhaps Scandinavian, defectors from the European Union. It is an idea which appeals to an identifiable body of opinion in both countries, although a much more significant one in Britain than in the United States. It builds on substantial historical experience. It brings together countries used to working together, as especially in the armed forces. And it looks to tomorrow's realities in a changing world as much as to yesterday's.

But it is not an idea that can seriously hope to fly. The United States wants a uniting Europe, not a fragmenting one. It could not welcome a British defection from the European Union. Of course it would not reject a relationship with such a Britain, but it could never be the privileged one which the advocates of the idea envisage. Britain would still be free to go buccaneering in the world, taking its chances where it could; but it could not hope to do so in convoy with the Americans, as a partner in an Anglo-Saxon alliance recreated out of wartime memories. And even if the idea did gather support in Washington as well as London, it is difficult to see it bringing any lasting satisfaction to the British. We would find ourselves in bed not with 14 European states and a European bureaucracy of which we form part, but with an arrogant and narcissistic superpower of 260 million people.

So a rediscovered special relationship with the United States does not offer Britons the escape from their European destiny which some of them still crave. More modest and realistic Atlantic roles for Britain are still demanding ones. In their interests as much as ours we need to go on reminding our continental partners of three interlocking truths. Europe must keep the Atlantic Alliance vital and relevant, with America fully committed to it. For Europe the view to the west is even more important than those to the east and south. And the European Union must remain open to the rest of the world and open therefore to the world community's single most important member, the United States. Our arguments will carry conviction only if we are firmly inside the European Union. If they fail to do so, Europe and North America will increasingly drift apart. The results will be disastrous for both, and particularly for Britain.

1   Raymond Seitz, *Over Here* (London: Weidenfeld & Nicolson, 1998).

2   See Samuel Eliot Morison, *The Oxford History of the American People* (New York: Oxford University Press, 1965).

3   World Bank report cited in *The Economist*, 23 December 1995.

4   Seymour Martin Lipset, *American Exceptionalism. A Double-Edged Sword* (New York: W W Norton & Co, 1995).

5   Robert B Reich, *The Work of Nations* (London: Simon & Schuster, 1991).

6   Lewis Lapham, *Waiting for the Barbarians* (London: Verso, 1998).

7   On this economic pre-eminence, and threats to it, see Michael E Porter, *The Competitive Advantage of Nations* (London: Macmillan, 1990).

8   Well summarised in a collection of essays originally published in Foreign Affairs, *The American Encounter. The United States and the Making of the Modern World*. (New York: Basic Books, 1997).

9   John F Kennedy, inaugural address, 20 January 1961.

10 For earlier views of the United States' situation in a world of weaker nations see Stanley Hoffmann, *Gulliver's Troubles, or the Setting of American Foreign Policy*, and *Primacy or World Order, American Foreign Policy since the Cold War* (New York: McGraw-Hill, 1968 and 1978).

11 For a scintillating analysis of the emotions behind the relationship and for a view on its prospects see Alex Danchev, "On Specialness" and "On Friendship: Anglo-America at *fin de siècle*", *International Affairs*, October 1996 and October 1997.

12 On the way transatlantic cooperation works in practice see Percy Cradock, *In Pursuit of British Interests* (London: John Murray, 1997).

13 Robin Renwick, *Fighting with Allies: America and Britain in Peace and War* (London: Macmillan, 1996).

6 The European orchestra

When the British want to decide where in the world they belong, most of them assume that they must begin with their neighbouring land mass, the place they call, depending on their predisposition, "Europe", "the rest of Europe", "the continent" or "Brussels". The European continent has mattered to the British throughout their history; as Britain's world horizons have narrowed, the rest of Europe has come to loom larger in its collective consciousness; and in recent years the political wrangle about the future of the European Union has gradually crowded out most other discussion of Britain's international concerns. The conviction that the Union is central to Britain's relations with its neighbours and an essential element in its future runs right through this book, but Britain's interests in the continent are far more diffuse than its connections with the European Union alone.

Let us look first at our links with Europe as a geographical concept, a centre of world history, a dynamic force in today's world, and in itself a sometimes terrible and sometimes wonderful reality. The rest of Europe is, first, our neighbour. More and more of us take our holidays there, and each of us, even the most blinkered, brings back some enduring image of similarities and differences. Thirteen million tourists come here annually from the continent. In 1994 ferries shifted almost 6 million cars between British and continental ports. The Channel Tunnel adds its share to the congestion of the roads of Kent, as well as 6 million passengers a year on Eurostar. In 1993 nearly half a million Britons were living in other member states of the European Community, one in three of them in employment. Apart from the Irish diaspora, 300,000 other Europeans were living in Britain, half of them working here. Millions of Britons know their way around a continent which, a hundred years ago, had seen us only in the form of Grand Tourists, wandering scholars, the first Cook's expeditioners and licentious soldiery. To some degree the English language serves almost everywhere in Europe today, even beyond the Elbe, but a surprisingly large number of Britons profess to speak a European language with some degree of fluency. The continent is not isolated today, even when there is fog in the Channel.[1]

Intimacy is even more marked when it comes to business. Over 70 per cent of Britain's exports go to European destinations, and five of its six largest markets are European. The United States sells us less than Germany; Japan less than the Netherlands. American, Japanese and Korean direct investment, attracted by an English-speaking manufacturing base in Europe, gets all the press attention, but investment within Europe across increasingly irrelevant borders is massive. BMW-Rover, Deutsche BA and continental bank holdings in London join British-Dutch conglomerates like Shell and Unilever and the European aerospace consortia. The steady drip of European Union regulation and standard-setting goes on eroding the barriers that remain. Such links spell human familiarity too: a management elite, at home anywhere that business or banking calls, officials commuting to Brussels and politicians to Strasbourg, the British workers on German building sites and the truck-drivers consuming Europe's motorways. Painfully the east Europeans too are now getting into the act , hungry for Western employment as the immigrant Irish were in the 19th-century United States.[2]

So everyday familiarity has moved beyond the caricatures created by populist politicians and the tabloids. The man in the Birmingham street dislikes what he hears about Helmut Kohl's high-handedness, but it is a dislike as much of politicians as of Germans. There is an animus against the Greeks and Italians who seem so gaily to bend Europe's rules, against French farmers burning English sheepmeat and Germans demanding the banning of British beef. But vulgar, undirected xenophobia is yielding to familiarity, and even the Europhobes are learning to turn their animosity against Brussels officials, condemned as bureaucrats, rather than against Europeans, condemned as foreigners. Another

50 uninterrupted years spent drawing the nationalities of Europe to-gether in their business lives, their holidays, their everyday routines, will disarm eastern European animosities as surely if as slowly as they have reconciled westerners to one another.

But a Europe without animosities is a difficult concept to accept, be-cause they form a central part of its story. Much of that story is a his-tory of war, and war sticks in the memory when good neighbourliness does not. As Norman Davies reminds us, Europe's heroes are national heroes revered for their frustration or destruction of other nations.[3] Britain always thought of itself as part of Europe but formed itself by differences from its continental neighbours; and all the countries of Europe have done the same. The celebration of difference easily dete-riorates into animosity, and animosity can lead to war. Yet Europe's differences have always been enveloped in its similarities. Voltaire started his history of the war of 1741 with the words: "I have always considered the Christian powers of Europe as one great republic, whose parts all correspond with each other, even when they endeavour at their mutual destruction".[4] Gibbon made the same point: "It is the duty of a patriot to prefer and promote the exclusive interest of his na-tive country: but a philosopher may be permitted to enlarge his views, and to consider Europe as one great republic, whose various inhabi-tants have attained almost the same level of politeness and cultivation."[5] And to the Italian novelist Alberto Moravia, writing of a continent broken by the Second World War, its cultural identity was "a reversible fabric, one side variegated, the other a single colour rich and deep".[6] European countries have always recognised both similarities and differ-ences, whether they called the things they had in common Christen-dom, the Concert of Europe or Western civilisation.

For 40-odd years West and East treated Europe as artificially but per-manently divided. The free world denied that it accepted the perma-nence of the Iron Curtain, and Germany in particular went on asserting the essential oneness of the divided fatherland.[7] But in fact the West accepted the reality of division and got ahead with building a converg-ing Europe in its western half. To the rulers in the East it was the socialist world, not Europe, which would come in time to supersede nationhood. It was only their peoples, voiceless but dissatisfied with what their half of a divided Europe offered them, who clung to the idea of a pan-European future.[8]

The completeness of the change which came to Europe in 1989 reminds us that we cannot afford to be determinist about its future. So does Europe's history. There was, after all, a time when Napoleon came close to uniting Europe under his eagles. For the 100 years that led to the First World War, it seemed destined to advance to ever higher levels of civilisation. Hitler promised the Germans European hegemony. NATO delivered security for half a century. The European Community helped bring prosperity to western Europe, and now most of eastern Europe wants its blessings too. But its future is no more guaranteed than was that of Napoleon's creation, or Hitler's. Fernand Braudel reminds us that "History sooner or later takes back her gifts".[9] Europe's prospects need to be examined with an open mind, without presumptions of an inevitable destination.[10]

❧

Historically Europe has had no single centre of gravity, but if we want to look at Europe as if we were playing the game "Diplomacy", Berlin is the place to begin. Russia, France and Britain have their permanent Security Council seats, but with its 80 million people and an economy twice the size of Britain's, Germany has a greater economic weight than any other country in Europe and an effective balance of economic and political assets. After 50 years of exemplary behaviour it has put its terrible past behind it: today's Federal Republic has got moral gravity too, and a growing political self-confidence. Its neighbours view it with respect, if with unexpressed but enduring memories of its past and a visceral anxiety about its potential. All of us, Europhobes or Europhiles, have to recognise that whether we are inside the European Union or out, Germany is going to have a major say in our future.[11]

But Germany also has its uncertainties. The economic wonder that was postwar Germany has gradually become an inflexible giant. Completing reunification is a task for the decades. Its political leaders maintain as an objective the Treaty of Rome's "ever closer union of the European peoples", with no inhibitions about the implications of a process that could lead one day to a Federal Republic of Europe. They see it as resolving the age-old problem of a Germany at the heart of

Europe, for Germany's benefit and the benefit of all its neighbours, east as well as west. But to an increasing number of Germans, "ever closer union" is yesterday's agenda, an irrelevance in a globalised world. Other Germans feel that the drive towards a European Germany risks undermining the postwar German achievement which the Deutschmark represents. There is much riding on this intra-German struggle, not least the continent-wide argument between a Europe of cooperating nations and the goal of ever closer integration.

Germany's western neighbours could, if they were of one mind, be a match for it. Together, the economies of Britain, France and Italy are half as big again as Germany's, and they have perhaps a better chance than it has of adapting successfully to the post-industrial world. British and French politics and diplomacy share a flexibility and a global view which Germany's lack. But the cards lie differently. Ever since the Treaty of Rome was signed, Germany and France have maintained a symbiotic relationship which has withstood 40 years' distractions. It gives both parties what they want: a guarantee of peace between them and in Europe, and a shared leadership of the European Union. Germany or France would have to go seriously and permanently awry before one turned its back on the other.

They show no signs of doing so, for while the second partner in the axis on the Rhine has an agenda of its own, on fundamental issues it does not seriously conflict with Germany's. Both are proud nations, France seeing itself as *the* European nation, now realistically content to lead Europe in partnership rather than alone. Like Germany it has its economic problems and a deep-grained reluctance to face up to them. Its leaders, like those of Germany, see the challenge of engaging their electorate in the European Union process as achievable, although they too will trim to their domestic political winds if they have to. And where the interests of France and Germany diverge – over differing economic priorities and over their respective preoccupations with eastern Europe and the Mediterranean, for example – they see a better chance of getting most of what they want together than separately. The relationship has been under strain recently, but taking the long view both parties are satisfied with the way events are moving. Together they can take the lead in shaping future developments, for they really do sit at the political heart of Europe.

The Netherlands, Belgium and Luxembourg were present at the Community's creation and together make a significant force in today's Europe. Belgium and Luxembourg house most of the Union's central institutions; the Netherlands on its own is an important industrial and trading force. There is in each of them, as in all the smaller European countries, a residual resentment of Germany, and although their instincts are all far more integrationist than those of the British, all three sit more happily at a European conference table which includes a constructively engaged United Kingdom. But even taken together as Benelux their influence is small beside that of France and Germany.

Of the Mediterranean European countries, Italy is the most significant and the most enigmatic. Its cultural inheritance outweighs that of any other European country. It has as many people as France. Economically it is on a par with Britain, and a decade ago it celebrated the *sorpasso* as if it were the Feast of the Assumption. Yet Italy has always failed to make of all its parts a sum that gives it political effectiveness in everyday business. Analysts toy with the idea of an Italy playing a decisive role in a restructured European balance, but it has never achieved the coherence and cogency to do so. Its instinctive preference for tackling many problems at the European rather than the national level reflects an instinctive acceptance of this weakness.

Spain is a new and effective actor on the European stage, and in recent years has scarcely put a foot wrong. On one level it speaks, with Portugal and Greece, for an impoverished southern tier of the European Union, with calls on solidarity to enable it to meet European standards. But it has made itself much more than a mendicant state: it is well-placed now to argue southern Europe's political case just as much as its case for development. Together with France and Italy, it embodies Europe's Mediterranean concerns, to put against Germany's preoccupations with its eastern neighbours.

The last of the western Europeans are the Nordics, the old stalwarts of the European Free Trade Area: Denmark, which joined the European Community with Britain in 1973, Sweden and Finland, set free by changes since 1989 to move away from their traditional neutral place in the Nordic balance; and Norway, which has twice voted for isolation. Here are people who instinctively look at Europe through something like the same kind of spectacles as Britain. They want a

European Union which is open to the rest of the world, economical and efficient in its operations. They lean not towards federation but towards a confederation of independent states doing business together. But they are people too who accommodate themselves to what must be; they are unused to standing up boldly for a political belief in the hope of carrying the day in a major conflict of wills.

So a brisk canter round the western half of Europe reveals no government within the Union prepared to ally itself wholeheartedly with the scepticism about its future which still commands such allegiance in Britain. When we get into detail the picture is different, as we shall see in the next chapter, for all over Europe there are politicians and interest groups who see difficulty or downright folly in particular aspects of the Maastricht and Amsterdam agendas for tomorrow's Europe. Throughout western Europe, however, majority opinion sees a continued movement towards "ever closer union" as inevitable and mostly desirable. There are subdued fears of German pre-eminence, but with them a belief that the best way to respond to them is to help keep Germans good Europeans. There are technical fears of a single currency, whose standards are difficult to attain and which could, if it went wrong, produce economic catastrophe. There are suspicions that the European Commission has an overweening concern for theory and unnatural uniformity. In some quarters there is a feeling that the high tide of integration may have passed. But against all this, governments from Finland to Portugal are still vividly aware of the political, economic and social benefits that the further development of the European Union can bring, and uneasily concerned at what Europe might become if it abandons the star that it has followed for so long.

In their search to get closer to their western neighbours the countries of central and eastern Europe bring with them another range of concerns. Although they celebrate their recovered status as truly independent European states, they fear Russia and, to a degree, Germany. They see the solution to their problems in membership of NATO and the European Union. Poland, Hungary and the Czech Republic are close to achieving membership of the one and (with Slovenia and Estonia) have made gallant efforts to prepare themselves for the other. Others will find it more difficult to adapt to European Union norms, and some may find themselves excluded from NATO for good. There is the stuff of new divisions and resentments here. But all the countries of central and eastern Europe offer their western neighbours new, eager markets and a partnership with cheap labour to match the United States' Latin America or Japan's Asia.[12]

Russia faces western Europe with issues of a different order of magnitude. Its history is one of psychological uncertainty about its relationship to Europe. It has always felt itself vulnerable to outside pressures.[13] Since the 16th century it has sought empire, or security, or access to the world through westward expansion. In the 18th century it conquered a continent's length of space and resources, all the way from the Urals to Kamchatka. Under Stalin it defeated the historic German enemy, conquered half of Europe, apparently for good, and made itself a world power. But throughout its history it has never satisfied itself whether or not it is European, nor whether Europeans accept it as such.[14] Now, with the efforts of 70 years in ruins and its authority pushed back from the middle of Germany to St Petersburg, it once again has to decide how it sees its relationship with its European neighbours.

~

Britain, at the other end of the continent, faces the same question. Like Russia, it has always seen itself as of Europe but not fully in it, ambivalent upon its margins. For 50 years it was preoccupied by the division of Europe between communism and freedom, for 40 by the exact nature of its relations with the western end of the continent, and this latter question still preoccupies it today. Let us look at the underlying issues in terms of the principles that have always shaped its policy.

The Channel has always given the British the luxury of seeing themselves as distinct from the rest of Europe. They have been spared Poland's exposure to rapacious neighbours, the vigilance of "*Die Wacht am Rhein*", and France's eye fixed always on the blue line of the Vosges which for so long formed its eastern border. But this has never relieved them of the necessity of involvement in continental affairs. English armies quartered mediaeval France, Drake singed the King of Spain's beard and armies financed by Britain fought all over 18th-century Germany. The British fought in Spain against Napoleon's marshals, and against the Emperor at Waterloo. They held their quarter of the western front in the First World War and liberated Rouen, Brussels, Bremen and Hamburg in the Second. Two generations of Britain's military families spent the best part of their active lives on the north German plain. Yet between all these engagements were disengagements, a turning away from the continent and a search for other things. "Their history is full of alternations between an indifference which makes people think them decadent and a rage which baffles their foes. They are seen, in turn, abandoning and dominating Europe, neglecting the great continental matters and claiming to control even the smallest, turning from peace at any price to war to the death."[15] So Albert Sorel summarised the mystery of British policy towards the continent.

But there have always been principles behind this mystery. The first was to keep the mouths of the Rhine and Scheldt out of the hands of any major continental power, for which England fought the 16th-century Spanish, 18th-century French and 20th-century Germans. A second was to oppose anyone who sought continental hegemony, whether Philip II, Louis XIV, Napoleon, Kaiser Bill, Hitler or Stalin.

The British were always prepared to use naval power and financial subventions to keep continental ports open to their trade. In Scotland and Ireland the English were concerned to ensure that no hostile power ever established a lodgement on their northern and western flanks. Times have changed, but it is interesting to examine how healthy those principles look today, when economics and politics are more important than military considerations but geography and strategy still shape political instinct and reaction.

From the point of view of the traditionalist, it is not a pretty picture. At the mouths of the Rhine and the Scheldt, the Dutch and Belgians are committed to an ever closer union within the European family. France and Germany together head that family, and not all the wiles of British diplomacy are going to tempt them to divorce. If the European Union goes on advancing as the Community has for four decades, it will become at least an economic and monetary union and perhaps eventually a federation. Many British traditionalists do not believe that that will happen and if it does they want no part in it. But Ireland does, and an independent Scotland would. So it is not beyond the bounds of possibility that in the first quarter of the 21st century, England could find itself isolated on Europe's flank. Norway, Switzerland and Iceland might be of the company. So might Sweden or Denmark if they shied away from the full development of European Union into a federation. But none of these aspires to play a major role in international politics, and none has made it a principle of policy to avoid such a situation, as Britain has, for nearly 500 years. A European federation of which Britain did not form a part would represent the defeat of 20 generations of British policy makers.[16]

༄

This vision has taken us far from Whitehall's everyday dealings with Brussels and other European capitals. In that more mundane world, Britain has assets and allies. Let us look at the context within which Britain's European policy makers operate.

An abiding objective is to establish a position for themselves in all the negotiations about Europe, inside and outside the European Union, "at the heart of Europe". Their assets are Britain's political and economic weight as a leading NATO and European Union power; diplomatic agility; divided councils among their partners; and other countries' reluctance to alienate a Britain which, in itself and its contacts, brings balance and enrichment to Europe. Their main handicap is domestic opinion which, even after the rout of Tory Euro-scepticism, is more tortured in its view of Europe than that of any of the continent's other 40 states except perhaps Russia and Belarus.

Those reservations and concerns have tied the hands of Britain's negotiators ever since it joined the Community. The creation of the Single Market excepted, British negotiators have never been able to position themselves for any sustained period on the positive side in discussions of major European issues. In recent years the British stance has come to look like nothing more than spoiling tactics. Our European partners may have understood the constraints of our political arithmetic, but we have strained their patience mightily. So far, Labour has carried less conviction that it represents a new start in Brussels than it would like to believe. British negotiators have a great deal of lost ground to make up as the Union moves on from the Intergovernmental Conference of June 1997.

The complexities of the European Union's development cannot be separated from the broader fate of Europe.[17] When Helmut Kohl quoted François Mitterrand as saying, "The return to nationalism, that is war", both men were accused of unrealistic alarmism. Certainly war in the traditional sense of conflict between one state and another is unimaginable in western Europe today. The process of locking democratic states together through trade, administrative integration and day-to-day familiarity excludes the prospect of war between any of the present 15. It does not exclude a decline into sullen and bellicose resentments, between Spanish and English fishermen, for example, or the mutual resentments of immigrants and the unemployed, or terrorist movements like ETA and the IRA. Further east, even conventional war does not seem quite so unthinkable as it was a decade ago. Transylvania, the Lithuanian-Polish border, southern Slovakia could conceivably go the way of the former Yugoslavia. Still further east, where the former Soviet Union faces east-central Europe and the three Baltic states that made their escape from it in 1991, the possibility of war, still improbable, is not something to be excluded from calculation. And in some of the former Soviet Union's Caucasian republics, bloodshed is an everyday occurrence.

Even a more peaceful fragmentation has its dangers. Already those who set themselves to the next great leap in European integration warn of the dangers of beggar-my-neighbour devaluations by those who remain outside a single currency. Immigrants are seen as a threat to stability all over Europe. Racism makes common cause with nationalism: in France, for example, or in eastern Germany, or all over eastern Europe. If it loses its sense of advance to an ever closer union, Europe will be unlikely to build a happy and constructive concert of nations, replicating the old continent at its best. If we are at "the beginning of the end of the European dream"[18] there is a possibility of the rebirth of an uglier version of old Europe. Britain's first task is to support all those who fight to prevent that happening.

Its second task must be to ensure that Europe remains open to the outside world. That means in the first instance ensuring that the United States remains constructively engaged in European affairs, primarily through the Atlantic Alliance. As we have seen, the United States is uncertain, potentially isolationist, conceivably dangerous. It is a prime

British interest to keep the Americans actively interested in Europe, without conceding them a *droit de regard* that would only exacerbate transatlantic relations in the long run, and without appearing to act as an American stalking-horse.

Keeping Europe open entails also a broader political, economic and social engagement with an outside world which, in east Asia, threatens to outpace Europe in the next 20 years, and which elsewhere calls out for European investment, interest and aid. British and European statesmen say all the right things about this; they are committed to an open world trading system, to the encouragement of inward and outward investment, to meeting others' economic concerns halfway, and to help for the developing world. But they find themselves driven to temper the wind of free trade to the shorn lambs of special interests and vulnerable sectors; to protect Europe's cultural inheritance against its appetite for American imports; to tolerate the continuing distortions inherent in the Common Agricultural Policy; and to acquiesce in many of the statist and corporatist assumptions lingering on the continent. As east Asia enters into its full inheritance and some other developing countries enter the global market place, the demands to pull up the drawbridges around Europe will spread to a wider group than their present, mostly eccentric, proponents.[19]

Britain's third task is an apparently procedural one, which nevertheless serves a political purpose. It is to keep itself centrally engaged in every kind of European negotiation. If it does not, it will lose its influence over developments and be left an observer on the sidelines. As we have seen, it has ample assets on which to draw in discussing European business. But it is inhibited by the divergence between its neighbours' hopes for the development of the European Union, and hence of all Europe, and the press-fed scepticism about the whole business of so many British voters. Hence the government's need to finesse its way through developments in Brussels rather than tackle them head-on: a need less pressing for Tony Blair, with his majority, than it was for John Major, but a continuing inhibition nevertheless. It is a policy that does not look heroic in the performance, but it is better on the one hand than a surrender to the out-and-out integrationists against which the electorate would rebel, and on the other than a fatal withdrawal from the European game.

The British government might do more to lessen the pressures upon it by reminding the country of the benefits it has gained from what the Community has achieved so far. For Britain, the advance towards a Single Market is a palpable achievement, marking for many the summit of what the European Union should aim at. It is still incomplete, and the regulations needed to perfect it can meet stubborn resistance from vested interests. But it gives Britain, and all the 15, the largest single market in the world. It facilitates intra-European trade and investment, and it increases Europe's chances of commercial success in a competitive global economy. Britain is economically the stronger for it, both within Europe and outside. Yet its very success confronts Europe with the question "what next ?"; and the answer, "economic and monetary union and a single currency", arouses huge controversy – about its feasibility, its desirability, and its political and diplomatic implications. There is material here with which the prime minister and his colleagues can work if they will. They have the encouragement of their majority to set against their manifest fears of the hostility of the press proprietors. It is a task for sustained and courageous but subtle leadership.

⤳

If these are the tasks which face British diplomacy in Europe, how can it tackle them best? The Labour government can build on affinities with left-of-centre continental governments. Its hand is strengthened by an economic performance which for the moment is proving itself stronger than that of its partners. But Britain has many fences to mend, a record of negativism to slough off, and the continuing inhibitions on what it can say and do imposed by a domestic opinion still warier of European designs than any other public except the Danes. While Britain can improve its relations with both France and Germany, there is no real prospect of turning the Franco-German axis into a triumvirate. Italy and the Netherlands do not offer a satisfactory, alternative axis of their own. Most of the rest of the 15 take a view of Europe which, as we have seen, is closer to the orthodoxy of Brussels, Paris and Bonn than it is to Whitehall's. There is no alternative Grand Design or Grand Alliance of European nations waiting for Britain to espouse.

Instead it is going to have to put together ad hoc coalitions, with their composition varying with the subject matter. Some are obvious, and respond to national boundaries. Almost all the smaller nations of Europe, for example, quietly welcome the exercise of any British influence that balances Germany's. The Nordic countries want an outward-looking Europe which respects national differences, a Europe very like Britain's own ideal; and they share Britain's suspicions of a centralisation that leaves them politically as well as geographically on the margin. Germany shares Britain's industrial concerns, although it pursues in the social market and in a concession or two to corporatism a different way to address them than ours. France sees in Britain a politically and militarily serious power, able and willing to take a joint lead in tackling dangerous instabilities, as Germany hesitates to do. On these predilections we can build alliances, strengthening our hand in one European poker game after another.

There ought to be a central and eastern European dimension in British calculations. We never carried great weight in that half of Europe that lies uneasily between Russia and Germany. A forlorn alliance with Poland in the Second World War, British agents in wartime Yugoslavia, British troops in Bosnia today, none of these has given Britain a central significance in the region. It is Berlin and Brussels that hold out most of the promise to Poles, Rumanians and Czechs today. But Britain has three great advantages there. The betrayal of Czechoslovakia at Munich apart, it carries none of Germany's historical baggage. It occupies a central place in the Atlantic Alliance. And as long as it cares to use it, its voice is listened to in the European Union. Moreover, central and eastern European countries which have always pined after western European support in their historical squeeze between Russia and Germany would go more than halfway to meet a Britain ready to build bridges to them.

So Europe today holds as much promise, and perhaps danger, for Britain as ever. The dangers of the cold war are done, but Europe is a far more complex place than the continent which the Iron Curtain divided. Its states have reasserted their individuality and freedom of independent action. In the east, the determinism of "building socialism" has been shown up for the sham it always was. In the west, voices are raised to question the determinism of "building Europe". Europe is reshaping itself, but its future is unclear. The European Union seems to be central to the continent's destiny, but its future too is uncertain. Every kind of British interest is engaged in the debate about Europe's future. We turn to the details in the next chapter.

1 *Social Trends, 1996* (London: HMSO, 1996).

2 Peter Calvocoressi, *Resilient Europe 1870–2000* (London: Longman, 1991).

3 Norman Davies, *Europe: A History* (Oxford: Oxford University Press, 1996).

4 Voltaire, *History of the War of 1741* (London: J Nourse, 1756).

5 Quoted in Felipe Fernandez-Armesto, *Millenium* (London: Bantam Press, 1995).

6 Cited in Davies, *op. cit.*

7 For the story of the division of Europe and its ending see Timothy Garton Ash, *In Europe's Name: Germany and the Divided Continent* (London: Jonathan Cape, 1993).

8 Charles Gati, *The Bloc that Failed: Soviet-East European Relations in Transition* (Bloomington & Indianapolis: Indiana University Press, 1990).

9 Fernand Braudel, *The Mediterranean and the Mediterranean World in the Age of Philip II* (New York: Harper & Row, 1972).

10 Enrique Baron, *Europe at the Dawn of the Millennium* (London: Macmillan, 1997).

11 Andrei S Markovits and Simon Reich, *The German Predicament. Memory and Power in the New Europe* (Ithaca: Cornell University Press, 1997).

12 On some of the technicalities of enlargement, see Heather Grabbe and Kirsty Hughes, *Eastward Enlargement of the European Union* (London: Royal Institute of International Affairs, 1997).

13 For a vivid illustration, see Eisenstein's cinematic treatment of the Teutonic Knights in *Alexander Nevski*.

14 Geoffrey Hosking, *Russia: People and Empire* (London: HarperCollins, 1997).

15 I recorded this in my commonplace book 50 years ago but cannot trace its origin. A bottle of champagne to the first reader to track it down.

16 Jim Northcott, *The Future of Britain in Europe* (London: Policy Studies Institute, 1995).

17 See for example Hugh Miall (ed.), *Redefining Europe. New Patterns of Conflict and Cooperation* (London: Royal Institute of International Affairs, 1994).

18 Jacques Delors in "A Country Called Europe", BBC 1, 15 April 1996.

19 We have not heard the last of arguments about the dangers of globalisation such as those put forward by James Goldsmith in *The Trap* (London: Macmillan, 1994).

7 The diplomacy of Rubik's cube

We turn from the general to the particular, from broad-brush ways of looking at Europe to the specifics of Brussels. Our first problem is to trace a route through the challenges that obstruct the European Union today to its longer-term prospects. Politics, economics, psychology and society are all involved, as well as the arcana of law and established practice that shape so much of Brussels' business.[1]

In 40 years the European Union's architects and builders have achieved things unimaginable to earlier generations. Half a continent is bound together in political, economic and legal intimacy. Its business has been driven forward with consistency, repeatedly overcoming obstacles which, within a more conventional institutional framework, would have been insurmountable. Governments have played a full part, and while each has fought for its interests with a passion, most of the time they have done their best to reconcile them with the collective good.[2] No government except the British has for long started from the premise that, unless proved otherwise, what the European Commission proposes must be detrimental to its national interests. The Union's institutions have brought new systems and concepts into existence which still have no parallel in other groupings.[3] Of course there are grounds for criticism: the European Union is human and therefore fallible. But the passion of its critics is a tribute to the strength of the structure which politicians, diplomats and officials have erected in the course of 40 years' sustained hard work.[4]

But, as the second article of the Maastricht Treaty on European Union makes clear, the Union is not an end in itself. Rather, it "shall set itself" certain economic and social objectives enumerated in that article. It is essentially a way for Europe to lay its hands on peace, prosperity, security, understanding, development and influence, and to avoid a return to the worst of its past. The Union's achievement in delivering these things is not open to serious question. Nor is its success in accommodating most of the disparate needs of its member states.[5]

Yet despite this record there is no dodging the fact that the European Union today is in crisis. Old hands say that it has been here before, that today's crisis is no worse than last year's, or the crises of 20 and 30 years ago. But the critics are vehement. They assert that the Community has driven ahead too fast and left ordinary people behind, and that the European political classes have brought the populist, nationalist backlash upon themselves. They argue that the idea of a centralised union is a postwar concept which for decades served a useful purpose but which is now out of date.[6] A Europe no longer ideologically and militarily divided requires a new approach, which accommodates new doubts among existing members and makes it possible to bring central and eastern Europe into a less demanding fold. Preoccupation with Brussels' structure building distracts the eye from the more important economic realities that everyday business has created. It is cross-Europe commerce, not Brussels regulation, that is the true dynamo of the continent. Obsession with Europe blinds its more myopic devotees to vastly more attractive opportunities elsewhere: the Pacific today and the Indian Ocean tomorrow. The more moderate critics believe that enough is enough. The more extravagant talk about repatriating some powers to national capitals. A few diehards in Britain still talk about withdrawal.

There is another view of the crisis. The Union's course towards "an ever closer union" remains the right one. It has given Europe a sense of purpose that the cynical old continent used to lack. In doing so it has sublimated patriotism into something richer and more complex, a recognition of a European identity to put beside the nations. In America's old language, Europe has acquired a "manifest destiny". Like the cyclist, the European adventure cannot stop pedalling without falling off. A single currency and economic and monetary union are necessary to complete the achievement of the single market. Without them, competing economic policies will begin to erode the market, the

Social Chapter and the commitment to regional development and solidarity. Without agreement to go on developing the Union, it will be unable to enlarge towards the east. Its members will relapse into the same kind of competitive nationalisms which have already taken the place of the old Soviet monolith in central and eastern Europe. The achievement of a single currency is the test of the Union's vitality, the logical next step for an ever closer union. It will open the way to the future. Europe's crisis is only loss of nerve.[7]

You can accept either of these versions of the state of the Union or neither. But their existence, and the conviction of those who espouse them, are enough to give each of the technical issues that face the European Union a political dimension. There is no need to accept all the alarmism on either side of the debate, but noone disputes that the adoption of a single currency will mark a step-change in European history. Few doubt that enlargement, bringing in central and eastern European countries with very different backgrounds, will alter the nature of the Union. In the same way, larger numbers around the Commission and Council tables will make improved mechanisms for the Union's decision-making essential. There is the problem of the Union's democratic accountability in Strasbourg and in national capitals. And there is the issue of exactly what face the Union will turn to the outside world.

❧

A single currency and an economic and monetary union that work bring obvious economic advantages. We all of us get better value out of our holiday money. Industry and commerce, particularly small firms, escape exchange costs between European currencies still proportionately higher than those which the Fuggers charged when their packmules carried bullion over the Alps. A united economy can be run at a higher level of efficiency than 15 or 20 national ones. Employment and technological advance both get a boost. European business becomes more competitive in world markets. The Union and its member states take another step towards collective responsibility for the economic well-being of all. Economic and monetary union brings psychological and political benefits, a sense of togetherness in place of otherness. A

European passport is symbolism, European money is reality.

These are good arguments if you believe that economic and monetary union and a single European currency will work. There are many
who assert that it will not, or not yet. The United States created its
economic and monetary union out of fledgling states which mostly
used silver in their transactions. Noone in history has attempted this
particular trick with a paper currency to be used by sophisticated and
disparate countries not just in their domestic and bilateral transactions
but in a globalised economy as well. To try to run the German economy and the Portuguese in double harness is a tough assignment, far
harder, for example, than the attempt to couple the economies of the
north and south of Italy in the 1950s and 1960s. The requirements of
the convergence criteria are driving weaker aspirants into unnecessary
recession. Different regions of the Union need different economic
medicine, which would be harder to administer under economic and
monetary union, and the Social Chapter excludes the more brutal
purges. Once national economies are locked together in a single currency, only catastrophe can set them free; and the attempt to set them
free would in itself have a catastrophic effect on European business and
banking. Disappointed hopes would do vast political damage too. A
failure would wound those outside the experiment as much as those
within it, with only the pleasure of saying "I told you so" to differentiate the two.[8]

The British are famously prominent among those who point to
these dangers. Rhetorical commitments are all very well, but the
British assert that they ignore the many technical problems that have to
be resolved if the euro is to happen. Britain has its opt-out, and the
whole process might conceivably be delayed. But even if it is, the economic objections to this politically motivated experiment will remain.
Only the naive can imagine a European monetary authority giving as
much consideration to the needs of the weak as to the demands of Germany, deprived of its Deutschmark security blanket and insistent that
the euro must, at any price in terms of growth and jobs, be equally re-
sistant to inflation.

British sceptics have political arguments too. The key issues in the
management of any economy are political. They must respond, if only
at one remove, to the wishes of the electorate. It is bad enough that in-

terest rate policy has been entrusted to the Bank of England. How can we conceive of surrendering it – and so much more – to continental bankers and officials, taking their orders from an ideologically-driven group of men around Helmut Kohl? And the idea that the European Parliament in Strasbourg can create for itself the authority it would need if it were to make good this democratic deficit is manifest fantasy.

There is good reason to doubt the political judgment and sense of proportion of Britain's most talkative Eurosceptics, and indeed the electorate showed little interest in their arguments at the 1997 election. But it is difficult to answer arguments such as these head-on. The European Union is on the brink of a critically important leap. It may go wrong or it may bring great benefits. But it will shift significant powers from national institutions to Community ones. Members will be surrendering to others politically and economically important decisions. The peoples of Europe are going to find some key issues being resolved even further from their street corner than they are today. That is why a respectable case can be made for Britain exercising its opt-out, not for one parliament or two, but for keeps.

Yet in continental Europe a determination to carry the single currency and economic and monetary union to fulfilment prevails. Barring real accidents, most member states are going to embrace the euro, if not in 1999 then shortly thereafter. Not every country will meet the convergence criteria. Even those that do are in for a lot of economic aggravation. But you need to be Mr Micawber to base a policy on the hope that the whole horrible spectre is going to vanish down the hole where nightmares go at dawn.

So the substantial doubts of the sceptics have to be weighed against the fears and hopes of others who see things in more moderate, some might say less resolute, terms. Let us assume that the British government, while continuing to express its good will towards the project, stands on the opt-out into the first decade of the next century. Let us assume that Germany, France and a majority of member states go down the primrose path laid out at Maastricht. Tony Blair's aspirations to lead the European Union will have gone the way of John Major's. The pound will no more be free of the influence of the euro than it is of the Deutschmark. Economic decision-makers in Brussels will be faced with a stream of proposals flowing from the commitment to economic and monetary union. In fighting their corner, the British and other outsiders will be up against a hard core of states that have committed themselves where they have not. These states will not want to see the constraints they have accepted undermined by the indiscipline of the rest. They will want measures that impose discipline on the defaulters quite as painful as the single currency criteria.

No one can be certain of the solution to this Rubik's cube, but it seems likely to lead to economic and monetary union which will in time include Britain and its fellow sceptics as well as the continent's true believers. But those of us intellectually committed to that route must accept that current doubts about economic and monetary union are real, with genuine misgivings aroused by the eloquence of its critics. Some of the arguments of the Eurosceptics are unworthy ones. They do not all deserve the credence they receive. But they have made themselves a real factor in decision-making, because governments must carry the people with them and because it is unwise and wrong for a democracy to brush aside popular instincts about a critically important issue. The euro and economic and monetary union are more likely than not to prove themselves the right course for Europe in the 21st century. But the politicians in Westminster have got to carry the man on the Clapham omnibus with them.

~

Economic and monetary union will be a giant step forward for the European Union, but it will not mark the end of history. Its most immediate effect will be to produce a Europe more divided than before. When all the forms have been signed, Europe west of the former Soviet Union will consist of four categories of states. There will be those that use the euro; those European Union members that cannot or will not; all the current candidates for Union membership; and those few European countries that, for whatever reason, are unlikely to join it. In face of this collection, there will be a case for a prolonged pause for thought. But it was agreed at Maastricht that after the 1997 intergovernmental conference, the Union should turn once again to the question of its enlargement. By the time the euro becomes a reality, the negotiations with some at least of the central and east European states will be well advanced.

Let us look at enlargement in the first instance not in terms of process but of destination. All the candidate countries of central and eastern Europe have been conscientious in their preparations for the enlargement negotiations. The Czech Republic, Poland, Hungary, Slovenia and Estonia are economically stronger than Greece and Portugal were when they became members, and their political credentials are irrefutable: these are peoples who have bled for their democracy. Romania is stirring and Slovakia is doing well economically even if its democracy leaves questions to be answered. Behind come Latvia and Lithuania, whose political case for membership is enhanced by the manifest difficulty of meeting their security needs through NATO. Then there is Bulgaria; and the troubled successor states of Yugoslavia if they can deal with the political and human rights problems that consume their attention today. Admit even half those candidates and you have, perhaps by 2010, a European Union of more than 20 members. Extension into the former Soviet empire and taking in the laggards would still further strengthen the European Union's claim to be truly representative of the continent. Even so, large partly-European states like Russia and Turkey would be on the outside looking in.

Each of these potential members of the European Union presents a unique picture; but they raise a number of common questions. How far has each taken the process of political transition, in terms of democracy, accountability and human rights? Is its economy advancing towards the goal of private enterprise operating in a free market open to the world? How far has the individual state been able to integrate its economy with those of western Europe? What problems does it face in adapting to European Union policies, in a transitionary period and when the full disciplines of membership come into play? Is the applicant able to face up to the requirements of the Union's growing foreign and security policy integration? Are the leaders and the people psychologically prepared for the subordination of the full expression of nationality to the demands of Union membership? Each candidate's answers to these questions will be different. As the negotiations proceed, some will fall by the wayside and others may turn away as they see the full implications of membership. But most will persist and in time most will qualify for membership.[9]

They present existing members with difficult decisions. Their economies will require substantial transitionary concessions. For some existing members, if not for Britain, their exports represent serious commercial competition. They will make heavy demands on the European Union's structural and cohesion funds, intended as they are to support its weaker members. They will dilute some of the cohesion achieved among the 15, just as British membership diluted the achievements of the original Six. Their accession will demand fundamental reform or abandonment of the Common Agricultural Policy. And the increase in numbers will make the management of the Union's business in Brussels, Strasbourg and Luxembourg that much more difficult. Just as there are those within the European Union who balk at the demands posed by the single currency and economic and monetary union, others will balk at the demands of these further enlargements.

But to those who believe that the European Union must be prepared to serve all Europeans, the difficulties are worth the candle. Membership will give the central and eastern European states a sense of belonging once again to the European mainstream. Enlargement can bring them prosperity and stability. Union membership will give countries like the Baltic states, which are unlikely to achieve NATO membership, virtual if not formal security guarantees and an alternative Western grouping to aspire to. Enlargement, with all its problems, will at last make central and western Europe whole.

⌒

The prospect of enlargement intensifies a problem which already confronts the 15. It forms part of a long-running and obscure debate about the need to "deepen" as well as "widen" the European Union. Let us examine it here under the rubrics of "governance" and "management".

The European Community has always presented problems of governance and management to its members and to the Commission. Its very nature takes it into subject areas and into degrees of detail which are absent from more traditional international groupings. Its patterns of work are intense (bringing some ministers together on a virtually weekly basis) and its ambitions are unlimited (the advance towards an "ever closer union"). There is a general recognition that reforms are needed, if little agreement yet on what form they should take.

The first problem is the decision-making process, both in the Council of Ministers, with whom most decision-taking powers rest, and elsewhere. As a regular gathering of foreign ministers, and in the form of meetings of ministers representing almost every functional responsibility of governments, the Council of Ministers deals with a bewildering mass of business. In it, national interests and the interests of the Community are reconciled or collide. Very frequently, the Council of Ministers cannot reach agreement. The issue, often a technical one of great complexity, gets referred to the heads of state or government in the European Council. As a result, what should be a periodical strategic summit becomes overloaded with detail. Throughout, ministers and prime ministers are conscious of their domestic electorates. The easy way to please them is to come home with what look like national "victories" for the Sunday papers. But in Brussels the machine that is meant to produce outcomes satisfactory to all has to turn in the following week to the next challenge, and the month after to the next. It groans, and in an enlarged Union would be impossibly overloaded. Hence the unending debate over majority voting. Britain has its own hesitations about its impact on its own national interests; but if it wants a more effectively governed and managed Union, more majority voting (or more often the prior resolution of disagreements which majority voting provokes) seems inescapable. So does a collective commitment to greater self-discipline in debate around the expanded conference table.

A second problem focuses on the post-enlargement size of an already over large Commission. Its present composition – two Commissioners from each of the major member states, one from each of the smaller – produces a Commission of 20. There are not enough real portfolios to go round and individual commissioners are tempted to make their mark by the very over-activity which provokes such resentment in the man who finds his beer harmonised by distant Brussels regulators. The answer here, much pressed by Britain, is for the Commission to do less but to do it better. But the problem of the size of the Commission remains. In a Union of 20 countries or more, its present composition would produce a quite unmanageable body. In the interests of efficiency and economy, Britain has to commit itself to changes which will almost certainly entail the loss of one of two British commissioners.

Britain also has to fight for discipline about the Union's languages. All national languages have equal rights in the translation stakes, and in principle in interpretation also. But in practice English and French prevail in almost all the Union's oral business. The threat comes from German, demanded on the basis both of Germany's own importance in the organisation and of the language's standing among the central European applicants. But if German asserts itself, so will Italian; and if Italian does, so will Spanish. The tower of Babel lies at the end of that road. Britain must fight for the status quo, and prove its good faith by doing what it can to stop the steady erosion of French as the Union's second language of everyday business.

Members of the European Council and the Council of Ministers are severally answerable to their national parliaments. The Commission is collectively answerable to the European Parliament at Strasbourg. To bring better governance and stronger democracy to the Union's business, two things are needed: regular discussion in national parliaments, and a more muscular and rigorous European Parliament. On the former, the British parliament usually does relatively well (the recent excesses of the Conservative Europhobes being defined as abnormalities) and exercises a supervision of Union affairs more effective than that of most of its fellows. On the latter Britain has always been ambivalent or negative, fearing what a stronger European Parliament might do or appear to do to national interests within the Union. But good governance is essential to good management; and good governance demands effective collective parliamentary oversight. If Britain is in earnest about building a more efficient European Union and subjecting the Commission to proper supervision, it must overcome its doubts about a growing role for the parliament at Strasbourg.

∽

There remains the question of the face the European Union turns to the outside world. The formal position is clear. The Maastricht treaty, which superimposed the European Union on the existing Community, gave it a "three-pillar" structure. The first was composed of the entities and treaties which composed the Community. The second created a Common Foreign and Security Policy. (A third, irrelevant here, concerned cooperation in home and judicial affairs.)[10]

The formal creation of a Common Foreign and Security Policy was preceded by more than 20 years' development of intergovernmental cooperation: Political Co-operation or "Poco".[11] It was explicitly co-operation, not integration, and the individual states remained predominant. It produced real advances towards ever closer coordination in this most sensitive area, but it repeatedly encountered factors that pulled the other way. One was the divergence of national interest and national perception. Another was the often competing attractions of the Atlantic Alliance and the United States. When foreign policy and security cooperation made progress it was by accommodating these factors. The same is now true of the Common Foreign and Security Policy.

Britain's position in all this is more important and more delicate than that of most of its partners. It has always accepted and valued the political nature and vocation of the European Community. It wants to enhance Europe's voice in the world. It values effectiveness in foreign policy and security. But it pursues a global foreign policy of its own, with an all-round efficiency that exceeds that of any of its Union partners. It values its links with the United States and sees a continuing and flourishing Atlantic Alliance as central to Europe's and its own well-being. So the Common Foreign and Security Policy is going to demand of Britain's political classes as much energy, good will and good judgment as the single currency debate, enlargement, and the reform of the Union's structure and working methods.

⤺

What kind of Union does Britain want? In early 1998 it is still difficult to be sure. The 1997 election saw the rout of a Conservative Party which had torn itself apart over Europe, and hence the most virulent of Britain's Eurosceptics. It saw the return to power of a party which professed to seek a positive, open-minded role in Europe. But these results do not eliminate doubts about the Union and its destination. They do not open the way to any committed pursuit of the course on which majority opinion on the continent is set: the further development of the European Union on out-and-out integrationist lines. Indeed, within a week of Labour's election victory the Foreign Secretary issued a mission statement notably spare in references to the European Union. It committed the Foreign and Commonwealth Office to "a global foreign policy", the first of whose strategic aims was "to make the United Kingdom a leading player in a Europe of independent nation states".[12] This suggested that in practice the new government would look at Commission proposals with quite as beady an eye as its predecessor, a suspicion that has been borne out in practice in the run-up to the 1998 British presidency. As this book goes to press the balance and outcome of that presidency remain unclear. But whatever the outturn, the Union seems likely to go on developing in its present way, two steps forward, one step back, confronting British policy-makers with the need to make choices which will affect not just the individual issue under discussion but the broader development of Europe.

A few snapshots of the way ahead illustrate the kind of choices they will face. The first, taken in 1999, shows the beginnings of a single currency union. A second, of the same date, shows negotiations for enlargement to the east, and, therefore, the beginnings of an even more disparate European caravan. Five years later, by 2004 or thereabouts, our snapshot shows a different Union, with a coalition around France and Germany fully committed to economic and monetary union, doing its everyday business in euros. Other member states will be trying to qualify for inclusion in that grouping. The new recruits from the east will still be working to adapt to its rigours, getting ready for full acceptance of the Union's agricultural and other disciplines and, much further down the track, for entry into economic and monetary union. Other eastern European countries may still be locked in accession negotiations in Brussels. So there will be as many classes of European Union membership or candidacy as on the old London and North Eastern Railway.

2010 lies beyond the range of conventional forecasting and the snapshots are blurred. But even though the gaps between the richer and poorer of the present 15 and between the 15 and the new entrants will not be closed, there is a good chance that they will be closing. By then economic and monetary union will be well established and beginning to reconcile economic disparities between its members. Its powers of attraction will grow with its successes. But national classifications will still be important within the larger Union. By political and economic power, population and interest, it is safe to assume that four countries will still stand above the rest. Italy will be one of them, even if it is still failing to put its strengths to effective use. France and Germany, each strong in itself and stronger in association, may still predominate. Britain will have its place among those four, the more assured if by then it has committed itself to the euro and economic and monetary union.

If Britain, 25 years after its accession, can now commit itself whole-heartedly to the development of the European Union, it will be well placed to take a lead in its councils. Our painful efforts to liberalise the British economy lend us authority. In most matters external to the European Union our contacts give us an advantage. And in the fields of security and defence we have a central position, with contacts and material assets to lend weight to our opinions. So we can if we will influence the development of the European Union, as it continues to make Europe a safer and more comfortable place, in which each of its parts is more at ease with its neighbours. We shall see the completion of the single market, the consolidation of economic and monetary union and the emergence of a European identity fully recognisable to the rest of the world. It will increasingly make an impact on the man and woman in the street. The sense of common identity, already a reality among the more mobile classes, will become more extended. A Sicilian peasant and a Laplander may still find it difficult to make much common cause, but for many others there will be a spread of everyday things in common.

The euro will unite people, with national currencies remembered for their quaintness as shillings and half crowns are today. Our high streets will resemble each other still more closely. So will taste in food, in clothes, in gadgetry. Language will increasingly become the main distinction between Europeans in their everyday lives. We will all be more polyglot, but not as polyglot as all that. English will have emerged as the main official European language, in the face of French opposition, with German throwing its considerable weight about to little real effect. Something will be lost in the process, with the lost national characteristics of those high streets or the forgotten glories of French provincial cooking. But much will be gained, as all of Europe gains access to the old continent's still infinite variety. For a present-day example, look to Prague, liberated less than a decade ago from the isolation of its communist past, overrun now by the tourists who take the edge off its glories but who gain an experience that speaks to them both of the city's meaning today and yesterday and of all of Europe's history.

Twenty years from now the European Union will still be an organism that spends an inordinate amount of time in defining what it is, what it is doing and under what rubric it is doing it. But since its beginnings, the essence of the Community has lain as much in process as in position, a process that began in Messina and leads wherever its participants decide it should lead. This characteristic will be as central to the European Union in 20 years time as it is today. It is this which makes Europe's work, tedious as it may be, an adventure, and it is this which quite understandably frightens those who lack confidence in it.[13]

~

Those who live within the European Union are made unremittingly aware of its weaknesses and disagreements. Outsiders increasingly recognise its strengths. To the candidates for membership its attractions are obvious, its problems things to be overcome. The United States sees in it the single European pillar and voice it has long called for. For east Asia it is both rival and partner, and Europe's best hope of organising itself to play an effective role in a world that will be increasingly dominated by the countries of the Pacific. To the developing world it is an important market that with vision and generosity could make itself more welcoming; a major investor and the biggest source of development assistance; and a factor of increasing political significance.

The Union brings Europeans advantages in the outside world. The first is a reasonable balance, at last, in relations with the United States. The story of the Atlantic Alliance is littered with experiments that were supposed to correct imbalances between the superpower and its weaker and divided friends. None of them ever came to much. The European Community by contrast has told a continuing success story, steadily increasing its range, competences and cohesiveness. Today the European

Union offers the United States a powerful associate: no superpower, no United States of Europe, but an organisation capable of shaping the continent and keeping its peace. It is capable too of playing a role beside the United States in many of the world's trouble spots, in a way that Japan is still unable to do. The void between potential and performance still yawns, as the early years of the Bosnian tragedy illustrate. There is ample scope for cross-purposes between a Europe still slow to organise itself and an America more uncertain in its international role than ever. But there is a vocation for the European Union here, and one in which Britain is on the whole happy to engage itself.

Europe's political relations with east Asia are still tenuous. When the flags come down in Macau, its last expression in real estate will be gone. If east Asia presents the world with its next great political crisis, Europe will be indirectly affected. If war were to come in the area, perhaps in Korea, it is hard to see European troops playing a part, even under a United Nations banner. But east Asia's economic significance to Europe is vast. Japan, China, South Korea, Taiwan, Hong Kong and the south-east Asian tigers are already centrally important in the world economy. Europe's task is to keep itself competitive with them. One way to do so is to learn from their successes and their mistakes. A lesson which the European Union may be able to teach in return is how to build a political and social entity which binds a region together, summons up new strengths within it and makes war in the end inconceivable.

Europe has interests and residual obligations all over the rest of the world. Islam affects it through the Arab world's troubles and propinquity; through the Moslem revival; and through Europe's own large Moslem population. Africa, ex-colonial neighbour across the Mediterranean, a continent deep in troubles, confronts Europe with immigrants, disease and environmental problems and calls upon its sense of responsibility and compassion. Latin America looks first to the United States, but with resentment; but Iberia has its special links with it and so have other European countries. Yet although the European Union has its instruments – its common external trade policy, the Africa, Caribbean, Pacific (ACP) relationship, its development assistance programmes and now its Common Foreign and Security Policy – the history of its sporadic involvements in the Arab-Israel problem, for example, illustrates just how far it has to go before it can offer consistent, coherent and collective propositions for tackling external problems.

Of all the world's trouble spots, the former Soviet Union presses most heavily on Europe. Russia, Ukraine and Belarus pose the old question that has haunted Russian history: of Europe, in Europe, distinct from Europe? They demand Europe's friendship and respect in ways that reawaken anxiety instead. How to deal with them depends on how they develop, whether hesitantly towards accountable government and market economics or back to authoritarianism. It depends too on their success or failure, perhaps following China into economic success, perhaps declining further into poverty and despair. But certain principles are clear. The European Union cannot afford to take Russia into its number; and if it cannot afford to admit Russia it should not admit Ukraine. But it must explicitly recognise that when it brings in the central and east European states and excludes these others, it is running a new line of division through Europe. So the European Union cannot afford to ignore any of these ex-Soviet societies. And although the United States' involvement is indispensable, to deal with the strategic capacity of its old opponent, for example, or to address the problems of Ukraine's nuclear remains, it is the European Union which has most of the assets and the major interest in these countries on its eastern doorstep. Its job in the east will not be done when, in the year 2010 or 2020, the last of the central and east European candidates take their seats in Brussels.

So the European Union has two vocations. One is to make sense of its own continent. The other is to project its common identity in the world. Britain has a choice between taking part in both or standing aloof. It can join in shaping Europe through the European Union and projecting it as a power for good outside. Or it can try to exercise its influence and protect its interests as a state on its own, semi-detached from the continent and its principal organising structure, making ad hoc alliances along the way. The first course involves the sacrifice of something of our sovereign freedom of choice, a freedom which is in practice more theoretical than real. The second makes of us nothing nor something, an opportunistic power. To me the right choice is clear; but all those who think like me have so far signally failed to elicit anything like enthusiastic agreement. So for Britain the choice is still open; it is the most critical we have to make in deciding our position in the rest of the world.

1   Ably summarised by Timothy Bainbridge and Anthony Teasdale in *The Penguin Guide to the European Union* (London: Penguin, 1995).

2   Christopher Tugendhat, *Making Sense of Europe* (London: Viking, 1986).

3   After 25 years of membership, there is still confusion in Britain about the European Union's main institutions. In a nutshell, they are as follows.

  • The Council of Ministers takes most of the decisions. It is composed of the Foreign Ministers, or as appropriate specialist ministers, of member states. It is supported by the work of the Permanent Representatives, who deal with the bulk of everyday business. It is serviced by the Council Secretariat.

  • The European Commission provides most of the European Union's civil service. Its President and Commissioners are chosen on a quota basis from member states, but serve the Union collectively, not the state from which they come. The Commission has the power of initiative in proposing European Union action.

  • The European Parliament is directly elected according to the electoral system in each member state. The Council has gradually given it increased powers, particularly over budget issues, but it still lacks the pervasive powers of most national parliaments.

  • The European Court of Justice supervises the compliance of member states with Union legislation, a particularly important role when it requires changes in established national practice.

  In 1974 another body was superimposed on existing Community institutions:

  • The European Council. This is composed of the heads of state or government of member states, and normally meets twice or three times a year. Despite the near coincidence of name, it should not be confused with the Council of Europe, which brings together most European countries, not just the 15, in its Strasbourg-based activities.

4   Stanley Henig, *The Uniting of Europe, from Discord to Concord* (London: Routledge, 1997).

5   Much of the route is traced in A G Harryvan and J van der Harst, *Documents on European Union* (London: Macmillan, 1997).

6   Karl Otto Pohl in "A Country Called Europe", *Panorama* BBC 1, 15 April 96.

7   For Europe's cross-purposes see John Newhouse, *Europe Adrift* (New York: Pantheon, 1997).

8   On the EMU membership issue see David Currie, *The Pros and Cons of EMU* (London: Economist Intelligence Unit, 1997).

9   Heather Grabbe and Kirsty Hughes, *Eastward Enlargement of the European Union* (London: Royal Institute of International Affairs, 1997).

10 The Treaty on European Union, in force from 1 November 1993.

11 S J Nuttall, *European Political Cooperation* (Oxford: Oxford University Press, 1993).

12 Foreign and Commonwealth Office bulletin, 12 May 1997.

13 David Smith, *Eurofutures, Five Scenarios for the Next Millennium* (Oxford: Capstone, 1997).

8   The pupils of Confucius

We look at the British now in the wider world to which discovery, trade and conquest took them. We start this exploration in east Asia where the world's centre of gravity in the next century may lie. In 1998 its financial difficulties attract attention, but they cannot obscure the region's past success and its long-term prospects. Economic achievement has already given the countries of east Asia political weight. It has also attracted attention to their cultural and social values. Geographically remote as it is from Britain, it is an area whose successes and failures increasingly affect our own well-being. Some see a case for attaching ourselves to it as closely as we are able.[1] Whether that case is right or wrong, and whether or not Britain could cling to Asia's coattails if it wanted to, east Asia's importance to this country is clear. So whereas ten years ago it would have been natural in a survey such as this to turn, after north America and Europe, to the world of Lenin, Stalin and Gorbachev, it is natural now to look to the Orient instead.

East Asia stretches from the Siberian Arctic to the Coral Sea and from the International Date Line to Mongolia and Tibet. China lies at its heart, by almost 300 million people the most populous country in the world and the sole remaining major Communist power. Japan has created in the last five decades the world's second largest economy. The two Koreas, dangerously divided, are yet doomed to a kind of bitter intimacy. Taiwan is equally at fraternal odds with China. The tigers' success is now called in question, perhaps by growing pains, perhaps by something worse. The region also includes very different societies such as Cambodia, Laos and Myanmar. Australia and New Zealand are closely involved with it, as in a more distant but pre-eminent way is the United States. Not even a latter-day George Kennan could cover all the region's complexities in a "Long Telegram".

Nevertheless, a few typologies are possible. Politically China, Vietnam and North Korea remain Communist dictatorships. Indonesia offers dictatorship in modern dress and Myanmar dictatorship in uniform. Monarchy survives in a meaningful form in Thailand, Cambodia and Brunei, and in a grotesque Communist form in North Korea. Singapore, Malaysia, Taiwan and the Philippines enjoy different versions of guided democracy; Japan and South Korea democracy associated with strong social control. Economic rankings produce different groupings. In China, economic drive goes hand in hand with political authoritarianism, producing dramatic growth in this huge society. Japan has led the way to economic transformation, with South Korea, Taiwan and Singapore following, and Malaysia, Thailand and Indonesia close on their heels. Vietnam and the Philippines have begun to emulate these tigers, while Myanmar, Laos and Cambodia are scarcely beginning to emerge from far more primitive conditions.

Most of these societies are ethnically mixed, with economically powerful Chinese minorities in many of them and with tensions which the outside world easily overlooks between the dominant peoples and indigenes. Crime, corruption, formalised prostitution, drug production and trafficking infect several of them. Each in its different way is characterised by religious or religion-related systems of belief and practice: Shinto in Japan, Islam in Malaysia and Indonesia, Catholicism in the Philippines, Buddhism in Myanmar and Thailand, Confucianism in Singapore, and Marxism or what is left of Marxism in North Korea, Vietnam and China.

But despite the financial typhoons which struck the region in 1997, its most salient features remain its economic achievement and its economic promise.[2] Many explanations of this success are on offer, some of them extending well beyond conventional economic analysis. The most persuasive appear to apply unbroken through most of the region. They include an attitude towards society that sets east Asians apart from their competitors, partners and fellow children of God in other parts of the globe. Hundreds of millions among them may be Moslems, animists or Christians, and hundreds of millions more may reject any in-

heritance from Confucius. Nevertheless, it is not entirely fanciful to at-
tribute some of the characteristics of east Asian societies to Confucian,
or perhaps post-Confucian, influences.

The first is widespread respect for authority, in the family, the company or the nation. A second is a general acceptance of the debt the individual owes to the community or family. The third is dedication to
self-discipline, education, training and hard work and the fourth
hunger for success and material well-being. Even when you have made
allowance for manifold exceptions, these qualities seem to lie somewhere near the root of east Asian economic success. They form the
basis of social and political systems which, flawed as they are, can look
westerners' very different values and attitudes in the eye.[3]

On the back of these qualities the east Asian countries have come
from nowhere in the last half-century. The Second World War left
much of the region in ruins as comprehensive as Europe's, and at least
one member of the British Colonial Service in the 1940s thought that
Jamaica had better economic prospects than Hong Kong. Since that
time the Japanese have built an economy more than two-thirds the
size of the United States' and more than twice as large as that of
united Germany. China's economy has grown consistently at 10 per
cent per year for the last decade. The economic performance of the
tigers has astonished the world, just as their financial problems are
now the focus of its attention. In the 1980s the colony of Hong Kong
succeeded in reversing the natural order of things by investing more
in metropolitan Britain than Britain was investing in Hong Kong.
Like Singapore, it has overtaken Britain in terms of GDP per head,
and if ever Malaysia does the same there will be self-congratulation all
the way from the Thai border to the Strait of Malacca. Indonesia's
rate of economic growth and its 200 million people started to turn it
into another formidable force. Even Vietnam and the Philippines
seemed to be invited to the feast.[4]

But now the region faces not the economic success to which much
of it has become accustomed but financial crisis, retrenchment and perhaps economic catastrophe instead. In 1994, Hamish McRae called east
Asia's achievement "the fragile boom", and the events of 1997 demonstrated his prescience.[5] It is still unclear whether Thailand, Malaysia,
Indonesia and South Korea can confine the damage essentially within

their financial markets or will see it spread to cripple first their economies and trading prospects and then to threaten the world's well-being. Japan, which should be the economic buckler and shield of east Asia, seems unable to take effective action. The region may be on the brink of economic catastrophe. If, on the other hand, the social and human qualities to which east Asia's success has been attributed live up to their reputation, it should in time emerge from crisis and go on to fulfil the promise to which its past achievement points.

But economic doubts and conceivable economic disaster apart, the face of the region is already shadowed by political and social clouds that could very quickly grow somewhat larger than a man's hand. If we are about to see a long-term reversal of the last decade's successes, Britain will share some of the region's pain, through the loss of investments, markets and sources of supply. And if the result turns out to be more grievous, putting an end to the story of east Asian success as fatally as the First World War put an end to Europe's rather similar 19th-century story, the shock waves will reach around the globe, with results as grievous as those of 1914–18. So Britain is quite as affected by Asia's problems as by its opportunities.

⌒

Japan's prospects are uncertain. In the last decade the Japanese have lost much of the drive and assurance which brought them success. Their economy, that miracle of industrial effectiveness, has grown more slowly than Britain's in the last five years and was mired in difficulties before the crisis broke in 1997. It may reassert itself as politics, banking, agriculture and society adapt themselves to the new world that Japanese industry has created; but its difficulties could be more permanent. Even on the more positive hypothesis, the Japanese will not find it easy to define their place in a world which their own success has so fundamentally altered. In the early 21st century they will face demographic difficulties, changing social attitudes and a high statistical likelihood of a major natural catastrophe. In a competitive world in which vigour, flair and imagination become essential to success, they may not succeed in shaking off the conventional discipline and conformity which have built their industrial empire. The story of Japan's next half century is unlikely to be that of the sustained advance which it has achieved since the Second World War.[6]

China's economic success has more recent origins and has further to go. Bring together political stability, hard-driving business management and a flight from the land in the most populous nation in the world and you have a formula for rapid economic transformation. It will continue to bring China growing economic power, the satisfaction of hundreds of millions of individual needs and environmental pressures whose solutions may fire yet more growth. At purchasing power parities, it may already possess the third largest economy in the world. In crude terms of size it seems bound to overtake Japan very soon and the United States early in the next century.[7]

China faces, however, a fundamental contradiction between politics and economics: the former strictly and centrally controlled by old men with attitudes shaped by the traditional Communist imperative of absolute control, the latter driven by the competitive instincts of Chinese business, both threatened by a pervasive corruption which even public executions are failing to deter. Only change can resolve the contradiction. China's economics lays its golden egg: to sacrifice it to politics would be perverse. Sooner or later, therefore, China's politics has got to change. But for 40 years Beijing has held down the pressure valve, consuming the political hopes of two generations in the process.[8] When it is released, the consequences will be unpredictable. They could be quite as drastic as those which Gorbachev set free in the Soviet Union and put in question today's straight-line projections of China's future.[9]

The Asian tigers are not confronted with such a stark choice between political control and market economics. Their current financial and economic difficulties may set them back decades, but from the thick of them they can still discern vast opportunities. First, to widen their industrial bases so that they can get their economies growing dramatically fast once again. Second, to use global free trade to enable them to satisfy the industrial world's appetites for their products. Third, to attract investment which will help them grow and at the same time enhance their status in the world economic system.

But they too face long-term political difficulties. In South Korea, Taiwan and south-east Asia, the consequences of past economic success and current turmoil threaten the political and social environment. Even Singapore is aware that its politics have not kept pace with its economics. South Korea and Taiwan are warily trying to make the political adjustment from authoritarianism to democracy. The contrast between economic achievement and political and social appetites is more striking in Vietnam and Thailand, in the Philippines and above all in Indonesia. Throughout the region voices are questioning authoritarianism and corruption, abuses of human rights and the absence of truly representative government. Other voices argue, with equal conviction, that the price of sustained economic growth is political and social discipline, that east Asia is fortunate in an inheritance of order and control that must not be sacrificed on the altar of western-style pluralism. Yet others point out that disciplined, regimented societies lack some of the verve that is essential to success in the post-industrial world. And the 55 million ethnic Chinese outside China's borders, themselves responsible for much of the region's success and producing more wealth than China itself, are vulnerable to the resentment that their economic success arouses among their non-Chinese neighbours.

Another doubt hangs over the region. It derives from the growing assertion of China's power throughout east Asia and from the absence of any effective Asian counterweight. The old men in power in Beijing have recovered Hong Kong peacefully but may yet feel compelled to use methods there which will shock China's neighbours. In the Straits of Taiwan they have threatened the use of force to support their assertion that the mainland and Taiwan constitute but "One China". In the South China Sea, they maintain far-reaching claims with scant regard for the fears of the south-east Asian countries, each of whose interests those claims affect.

So the uncertainties of China's policies suggest that the country's future may be one not of economic advance alone but of political aggrandisement and even conquest as well.[10] The anxiety affects Indonesia, 2,000 miles away, as much as South Korea, with its memories of Chinese invasion. The collapse of North Korea could provide a flashpoint. As its generation of ancients leave the political scene, China may need to divert attention from domestic difficulties to the South China Sea or Taiwan. If there is major armed conflict in the early 21st century, it is more than likely that it will occur somewhere in east Asia. Unimaginable as it may seem today, it could pit a nationalist China against a nationalist Japan.[11]

Asia lacks the elaborate cooperative machinery which has kept the peace in most of Europe for so long. National perceptions and interests are too much at odds to encourage any cohesive grouping. Stability throughout east Asia therefore still depends on the United States' involvement through the commitment in the US-Japanese Security Treaty of 1951 to uphold "peace and security in the Far East" and through the deployment of United States forces in the western Pacific from Hokkaido to Australia.

That involvement evokes ambivalent feelings in most Asian breasts. At the same time American preoccupation with domestic problems calls Pacific as well as Atlantic commitments in question. Americans look at prosperous Asians and ask why they cannot defend themselves. After Vietnam, any American commitment to land war in east Asia is unthinkable.[12] In the region, even more than in Europe, there are no easy answers to the problems of post-cold war security. Japan should play a central role in securing peace and international discipline in Asia; but half a century after Hiroshima it remains inhibited when it comes to matters military, and it is politically ill-placed to take the burden off American shoulders. If Japan were to overcome its doubts about deploying large forces abroad, as it would have to do if American disengagement were to leave China otherwise unchallenged in the area, it would be seen by its neighbours as posing a new problem quite as much as helping to meet an old one. Thus the US-Japanese security relationship serves the interests of both parties and of the whole region. It seems unlikely that either would throw it away, as the Philippines rid itself of United States bases in 1992. Yet it has never been an easy relationship, and discontents about it infect other aspects of cooperation between the Americans and the Japanese.

The most important of these discontents concerns trading relationships between the United States and east Asia. The emergence as successful trade rivals first of Japan, then of the Asian tigers and now of China bites deep into the American psyche. There is a conviction, part factually based and part fictional, that Asian markets are too closely guarded against American exports; that Japan is buying up the United States; that Asian industrial success stands on a basis of sweated, juvenile or slave labour. These suspicions sometimes lead to a subordination of foreign policy to trade policy, to obsessions which unbalance both, and to unilateralism which conflicts with World Trade Organisation commitments.

The east Asians answer these American suspicions with suspicions of their own. They believe that United States policy in Asia is driven by commercial considerations and that Washington is too ready to use its political muscle to force the rewriting of trading rules. While they want to build some Asian identity of their own and an effective focus of economic cooperation, they suspect that the United States wants to frustrate their efforts almost before they have begun. Like the Europeans, they experience a steadily increasing resentment of what they see as American political, diplomatic and commercial arrogance, the more galling because they cannot escape America's indispensability.[13]

∽

Faced with all these doubts about the Pacific century Britain, in deciding its place in the world, must reckon with a peaceful, powerful and prosperous east Asia but cannot exclude the possibility that it may turn out to be a region of difficulty, peril and even disaster instead.

What have all these distant countries to say to the average Briton? He drives a Japanese car, she works in a Korean-owned company, and they enjoy their daughter's accounts of backpacking in Thailand. They have heard grandfather's tales of fighting the Japanese and father's of jungle patrols in Malaya in the 1950s. Their local Thai restaurant provides an alternative to the Chinese, and news of the latest Asian investment bolsters their faith in Britain. But for most Britons, China, Japan, Malaysia, Singapore remain psychologically as much as geographically distant. Australia and New Zealand are nearly twice as far away, yet for the British they are cousinly countries, exempt from ordinary considerations of time and distance. It is east Asia that is our psychological antipodes.

Yet Britain led the West's discovery of east Asia. Lord Macartney's trade mission to Peking in 1793 was the first such expedition in the modern period, just as the ruffianly British merchants of Hong Kong took the lead in probing China's weaknesses half a century later. Stamford Raffles made Singapore a port and opened the South China Sea to western trade, where James Brooke waged war on Dayak piracy and brought government to Sarawak. Throughout east Asia, British missionaries, scholars and aesthetes played their part too, as did colonial governments and little garrisons in the Malay States, North Borneo and Hong Kong.

Everywhere in east Asia there grew up British diasporas of merchants and seamen, planters, missionaries, diplomats and officials, reinforced by regular visits by the Royal Navy. If it never attained the significance of the British presence in India, it left a mark of its own on Britons who never travelled east of Suez: think, for example, of Joseph Conrad's and Somerset Maugham's explorations of the psychological interplay between Britons and Asians. The Second World War brought vivid experience of the collapse of a colonial world and white supremacy, the miseries of jungle warfare and the lethal brutalities of Japanese captivity. Those events broke British authority and confidence, and even after Japan's defeat there was no going back to prewar verities.[14] Experiences in the Korean war, in Malaya and in Malaysia were of a loose-end order. So, much more protractedly, was the story of Hong Kong.[15]

There is a similar story to tell in Britain itself. In the 19th century Chinese seamen started to impinge on the fringes of British consciousness. So today do Chinese restaurateurs. They connect only vaguely with an episodic awareness of China itself: of its huge population, dynamically expanding market and human rights abuses, of Tibet and of Tiananmen Square. Japan impinges in a different way, noted for its consumer goods of impeccable quality and for inward investment that has rescued entire British industries from collapse. These images are mixed with carefully nurtured memories of wartime atrocities, resentments of whaling and driftnet fishing, and a conviction that Japan's is an impenetrable and ultimately inhuman society. Awareness of the rest of east Asia is even more fragmentary, seeing it as a remote, inscrutable and scarcely comprehensible world.

So there is a limited historical awareness and some slight psychological underpinning to support Britain's interests in east Asia and hopes of building a more intensive relationship with it. Yet this is a field where the facts run ahead of the perceptions, just as in Britain's approach to the United States we have seen the perceptions running ahead of the facts. Britain has an important stake in east Asia. The Japanese market is worth £4.2 billion a year to Britain, the Chinese £700 million. Japan's investment in the United Kingdom is worth £20 billion. Five per cent of Malaysia's imports come from Britain, and as the human rights campaigners remind us, Indonesia is a major market for British weapons. There is no reason why British business should not win perhaps 3 per cent of the east Asian market which, barring catastrophes, is likely to grow at more than 5 per cent per year for the next 20 years.

What do east Asians think of Britain? Japanese and South Korean businessmen recognise it as the most accessible and flexible economy in Europe, a gateway to the continental market and a useful partner in economic enterprise. They and other Asians respect its experience and its political connections and have been impressed by its recovered economic liberalism and commercial dynamism. They have demonstrated their faith in it by their inward investment in Britain. But in Asian eyes it is a declining power in a stagnating region, insignificant beside the United States, economically Germany's inferior, and a country less at ease in Europe than France or Italy. In places where Commonwealth connections might be expected to help, as in Malaysia, there seems instead to be a persistent animus against it. Throughout the region there is no obvious basis for the proposition that Britain might build a position of particular advantage there.

Yet the idea persists, particularly in relation to Japan. In Japan and Britain today, observers ask whether more could not be made of the relationship between the two countries; to some Britons who are sceptical of their country's European vocation, a link with Japan, and through Japan with the wider Pacific region, has the makings of a political as well as an economic alternative. They point to bilateral trade of significance to both parties, to British experience of Japan and above all to Japanese direct investment in Britain, which has recreated the British car, consumer electronic and computer industries, deeply influenced the methods of every serious British company and eroded many negative stereotypes about Japan. It has brought other east Asian investment in its wake and given Britain an industrial and psychological edge over its European Union partners.[16]

The proposition is not a novel one. British and Japanese speech-makers used to talk in the 1950s and 1960s about twin offshore island kingdoms, building a special relationship together around the globe. It was always obvious that this must be a second-order relationship, coming behind Japan's preoccupations with the United States and with east Asia and Britain's with the United States and Europe. Since then the capacities of the two countries have moved apart. While Japan has thrust towards economic equality with the United States and to global authority as the world's biggest aid donor and third largest trader, Britain has disembarrassed itself of the relics of empire whilst trying to adapt to Europe and reverse its economic decline. Economically, Japan is by a considerable head the leading partner in this relationship.

However, the relationship is not just economic. Where Japan's strengths are predominantly industrial, Britain's lie in politics, in connections and in financial services. Japan has brought method, social cohesion and consensus to industrial success, and their corollaries are perhaps inflexibility, slowness of response and a stultified imagination. The British approach is personal, individualistic, self-expressive. Britain and Japan both have historic enemies who nurture resentments of what the empire and the co-prosperity sphere did to other races. In their efforts to win over those enemies, the Japanese deploy political diffidence and the practical assistance their economic success can bring. The British approach is different, basing itself on a developed sense of political responsibility, personal relationships and persuasion.

The optimists point to this complementarity and assert that there is more to play for. One possibility is cooperation in third countries, bringing together the contacts and experience of Britain's political strength with Japanese industrial muscle. Perhaps they share a perception of the global balance of forces. They both recognise the indispensability of the United States but the need to guard against its excesses. They prefer a cooperative to a confrontational approach in international relations and in world trade, with a respect for the international institutions and a desire to reinforce them. And although Japanese history in recent decades has been a story of spectacular economic success while Britain's is one of relative decline, events in the last ten years have done something to redress the balance. Add in Britain's political advantages and both countries at present enjoy about the same influence in the world. Some would take the proposal further, with the two countries doing one another purely political favours – in relations with the United States, for example, in the rest of Europe and in the developing world.

All this adds up to an intriguing but strangely unrealised series of propositions. There is everything to be said for bilateral relations with Japan which are as warm, close and substantial as effort on both sides can make them. They can help sustain and enhance economic cooperation between British and Japanese companies in the global economy. Such relationships will bring advantage to Britain in Asia and to Japan in Europe and Africa. They are also a hedge against the temptation on both sides of the Pacific to cut American-Asian deals that neglect the interests of third parties. But basic facts of politics and geography stand in the way of an attempt to build a politically ambitious superstructure on what is at present a useful relationship of convenience. Both countries have preoccupations nearer home which cannot be waved aside. Neither could sensibly commit itself to binding security obligations at the other end of the world: ask, for example, what Japan could usefully do to help Britain in a European crisis or Britain to help Japan in a showdown with China. And the fact remains that much of Britain's present value to Japan and east Asia derives from its membership of the European Union.

So Britain must cultivate a less ambitious relationship with Japan than the revisionists advocate. There is plenty to be done. We want yet more Japanese investment. We want Japanese help in achieving better results in the Japanese market. We can learn from Japanese industrial, economic and perhaps even social experience. We want to use whatever influence we have got to guard against collusion between the United States and east Asia at our expense. We value the contribution to stability which a Japanese presence and Japanese aid can bring to the developing world. We rightly encourage greater Japanese political and security commitment to global order, and sharing our own contacts and experience can play a role in that process. But Japan remains a competitor as much as a partner; a country whose record of success in the last 40 years looks unlikely to be sustained for the next 40; and a place which could find itself, as we saw earlier in this chapter, somewhere near the epicentre of the next great world crisis.

࿇

In its dealings with China, Britain faces quite different issues and the most profound potential contradiction of all its foreign policy options. It wants close relations with what will in time be the world's biggest market and a global power with a great capacity to help or harm British interests. But it hesitates to condone many aspects of China's policies, from its human rights record at home to a diplomatic and military self-assertion which threatens to disrupt the security of Asia. And in its attitudes towards China, Britain carries an additional burden, beyond those carried by its Western partners, for Chinese-British relations remain infected by the psychological consequences of the return of Hong Kong to China in 1997.[17]

Less than a year after that event it remains too soon to judge how China's policies and practices will develop in Hong Kong. It managed its resumption of authority decently, if with little grace. It has so far conducted itself properly there. But the world can only assume that any development in Hong Kong which the government of China construed as a threat to its absolute political authority would be crushed with all necessary ruthlessness. So the relative freedoms of Hong Kong depend crucially on the self-restraint of all those in Hong Kong who developed a taste for democracy in the last years of British rule. But Britain professes to recognise its moral and even political responsibility to ensure that China lives up to the commitments it undertook in the 1984 agreement. So British policy towards China will in a sense remain a hostage to the politically active classes it left behind in Hong Kong when the last governor sailed away. Only political change in China, forced upon its rulers by the contradiction between their economic liberalism and political authoritarianism, will set the hostage free.[18]

Meanwhile, economic success gives China self-confidence, material strength and a powerful position in bargaining with any nation that seeks access to its markets. Success reinforces Chinese resentment of criticism of Beijing's policies, particularly on issues such as human rights, Taiwan and Tibet which, like Hong Kong, it sees as exclusively its own affair. Nor will the Chinese leadership take kindly to criticism of, still less resistance to, Chinese foreign and trade policies which threaten regional or international stability. So Britain, like all its western partners, faces choices between foreign policy goals which cannot be reconciled. It wants its share of the fast developing Chinese market. It cannot lightly afford to alienate a world power of the near future. Yet a foreign policy which consciously seeks to promote ethical concerns over democracy and human rights can be called hypocritical every time it condemns abuses in Burma, Indonesia or the Arab world and passes over in silence far greater abuses in China. Britain, like its partners, will have to pick its way between all these considerations, doing its best to reconcile conflicting goals and achieve a kind of consistency in what it says and does.

For as long as China remains an authoritarian and politically reactionary place it will confront the internationally active countries with these dilemmas. Conscience, free speech and fear of what an unchecked China might become will continue to call on us all to criticise its record on pluralism, accountability and human rights and to give political support to American efforts to preserve security in Asia. Yet we will be made ever more aware of the value of Chinese trade and the political importance of China. Britain will have to factor into its calculations the complication of its remaining responsibilities over Hong Kong. So our relationship with China, potentially the most important country in the world, will remain a tentative one. Its importance to us will grow as China's strength grow. But it will remain a second-order relationship. The major power steadily becoming a great power will be far removed from us by geography, experience and *Weltanschauung* alike.[19]

↬

The rest of east Asia takes us into areas affected by colonialism in its classic form, which scarcely touched north-east Asia. Britain's historical points of entry to the area are Singapore, Malaysia and Brunei, together with relationships with Australia and New Zealand which still have something of a family feeling about them. With these countries too, it is argued, Britain should seek to build relationships of particular confidence, drawing on links that go back to colonial times. For example, distance does not prevent Britain being Malaysia's fifth largest export market, basing banking operations in Singapore, and protecting in

Brunei some of the most freely disposable personal wealth in the world. These countries, familiar for a century to British business, sit at the heart of the fastest growing region of the world. They may be examples of a new Commonwealth dynamism, on which a new Commonwealth relationship might be built, based on hope rather than on the more familiar materials of nostalgia, guilt and compassion.

The proposition is more attractive in conceptual terms than in practical ones. In the first place, historical and Commonwealth ties buy no manifest advantages in Kuala Lumpur or Singapore. Malaysia's colonial experience was gentler than that of many other members of the Commonwealth. It owes its existence to British help against its Chinese Communist insurgents and in its confrontation with Indonesia. But Malaysia seems driven, as India, Pakistan and the African Commonwealth are not, by an urgent passion to put the ex-colonialists in their place. "Buy British last" in Malaysia in the early 1980s was a policy that responded to the particular circumstances of the time, but it reflected a much more widely based resentment, whether justified or not, of Britain's record and attitudes. Malaysia and Singapore still see no advantage in doing Britain particular favours; and only a marginal interest in trying to re-weave the cloth of Commonwealth .

There is also a broader and more enduring consideration which stands in the way of this proposition. South-east Asia is driven by a desire to build regional organisations in a way that north east Asia is not. It wants to reinforce national self-assertion by cooperation. The Association of South-East Asian Nations reflects real ambitions and concerns. It expresses a sense of an Asian identity, the more intense because of past colonial humiliations; a desire to advance the region's interests as a participant in the "Pacific century" whose concerns might be overlooked beside those of Japan and the United States; and a little mentioned but very real fear of China. Malaysia and all its south-east Asian neighbours look first to one another; second to the great powers of Asia to the northwards; and thirdly to the Pacific, Australasia and the United States. Malaysia exports three times as much to Japan and five times as much to the United States as to Britain. In the last ten years the region has become intoxicated by rates of growth four times as fast as Europe, by the confidence that the world's tallest 21st-century skyscrapers will be Asian. The last year has shown that south-east Asian pride, like any other, goes before bruising falls, but to the region's movers and shakers Britain seems wearily old-fashioned by comparison with the targets that they have set themselves.

Australia, by contrast, is a near neighbour of the south-east Asians, and offers them some signs of dynamism to match their own. Its diplomacy has worked hard in the region in recent decades, and if racist politics within Australia do not throw the advantage away, the Australians stand well there. They have the beginnings of a particular relationship with some of the countries of the region, just as they have something of a particular relationship with Britain. Cooperative ventures with Australia, and to a lesser extent New Zealand, may offer Britain an access to a Pacific eldorado it could not achieve alone.

On its own Britain has no high-value political cards to play in its dealings with that eldorado. Its assets in its dealings with Malaysia and Indonesia, Thailand and the Philippines will be commercial ones: needed goods and services, effective investment, a market for the region's own goods and services. Commonwealth links may help a little; the English language will help more, as would a British education for the next generation of south-east Asian leaders. But all those things will seem increasingly marginal as south-east Asia grows more powerful: Oxford against Harvard, the Manchester market against Osaka, the presence of American protection against memories of a Royal Navy gone from the South China Sea more than a generation ago. The British can go on making an effective impact in this part of the world as businessmen who know there way around it as few other outsiders do. If they want to do more it must be by using their experience and contacts to shape European Union policies towards south-east Asia which win the confidence of people who, 30 and 40 years after independence, still nurse edgy resentments against the old colonial powers.

⌒

East Asia, therefore, does not offer Britain the prospect of waking up one sparkling Monday morning in a new place on the map of the world. The region is nevertheless self-evidently important to us. As its global weight increases, so will its importance to British statesmen, exporters and financiers, who will have to give increasing attention to east Asian views, interests and initiatives. The area may turn out to have an enduringly successful social and economic model to demonstrate to the world. But even if the model withstands the test of time in Asian circumstances, it could prove to be like a lighter wine of Tuscany drunk on a San Gimignano terrace on an idyllic summer evening, something that does not travel. We must stay engaged in east Asia, on as good terms as may be with the countries of the region, trying hard to understand them better. We must win what we can of their markets and their investments, watchful that any deal Asia and the United States cut between them is one that respects our interests. We will do all these things better in association with our European partners than in detachment from them.

1   See for example David Howell in "The Age of Asia: Learning from the Sunrise Societies", *Demos*, Issue 6, 1995.

2   John Naisbitt, *Megatrends Asia: the Eight Asian Megatrends that are Changing the World* (London: Nicholas Brealey, 1996).

3   See Vincent Cable in "The Age of Asia" above.

4   *The Economist Pocket World in Figures* (London: Profile Books, 1997 edition).

5   Hamish McRae, *The World in 2020* (London: HarperCollins, 1994).

6   Jon Woronoff, *The Japanese Economic Crisis* (London: Macmillan, 1996).

7   Greg Mastel, *The Middle Kingdom Emerges* (New York: Sharpe, 1997).

8   See for example the human tragedy documented in Wei Jingsheng's lifetime in prison in *The Courage to Stand Alone: Letters from Prison and Other Writings* (New York: Viking, 1997).

9   James Miles, *The Legacy of Tiananmen: China in Disarray* (Michigan: University of Michigan, 1996).

10 Richard Bernstein and Ross H Munro, *The Coming Conflict with China* (New York: Knopf, 1997).

11 John Boyd, "The Risks of Conflict between China and Japan" (unpublished paper delivered to an IISS/Yomiuri conference at Gotemba, Japan, in December 1996).

12 Robert S McNamara, *In Retrospect. The Tragedy and Lessons of Vietnam* (New York: Random House, 1995).

13 For wide-ranging background see Samuel P Huntington, *The Clash of Civilizations and the Remaking of World Order* (New York: Simon & Schuster, 1996).

14 Christopher Thorne, *Allies of a Kind. The United States, Britain and the War against Japan, 1941–1945* (Oxford: Oxford University Press, 1978).

15 John Keay, *Last Post. The End of Empire in the Far East* (London: Murray, 1997).

16 Anglo-Japanese Economic Institute, *Anglo-Japanese Collaboration: On to Global Partnership* (London, 1995).

17 Jonathan Dimbleby, *The Last Governor* (London: Little Brown, 1997).

18 Robin McLaren, *Britain's Record in Hong Kong* (London: Royal Institute of International Affairs, 1997).

19 Percy Cradock, *Experiences of China* (London: John Murray, 1994).

9   The people of the book

The last chapter took liberties with the significance of Confucius. There is no need for such liberties in this one, for the teachings of one man, the prophet Mohammed, run uninterrupted from Indonesia to the London Borough of Tower Hamlets. Nevertheless, it confronts us with the difficulty of teasing out those issues, distinct but inter-linked, which present themselves in a Moslem or a partly Moslem con-text and which have a direct bearing on Britain and its place in the world.

The first of these issues is the reason for breaking away from a purely geographical approach and devoting this whole chapter to the Moslem world. With over one billion believers, Islam is one of the world's great religions, commanding a loyalty and fervour which have largely van-ished from other faiths. It stands on strong theological, ethical and pas-toral bases and looks back to a glorious religious and intellectual past. Islam offers a model of thought and behaviour which has social and po-litical as well as religious implications. It is growing where other faiths are in decline. It may develop into something more at ease with the modern world than it is as present. Conversely, a world seeking to re-cover its religious faith could turn to it as a system of belief and prac-tice that has kept itself relatively untainted by material things.[1]

A second factor is the economic importance of many Moslem coun-tries. The Gulf and Saudi Arabia hold commanding positions in the world's oil markets. The Caspian and some of the predominantly Moslem republics of the former Soviet Union are joining them. The economies of the West depend on oil from Moslem sources. British oil companies are heavily engaged in many of these oilfields.[2] A collapse in the oil price, itself largely established by factors in the Moslem world, would drive British North Sea production out of business. The oil-rich are highly important markets for Western exports, particularly the major construction projects and arms sales on which the British economy is disproportionately dependent. Finally, as we saw in the last chapter, Moslem countries like Indonesia and Malaysia are developing an economic significance which extends beyond oil, into manufactures which challenge established Western industries.

The third issue is Islam's interaction with the West. From central Asia to the Straits of Gibraltar, societies with a greater or lesser degree of commitment to Islam are face to face with societies which think of themselves as Christian or post-Christian. Both look back on historical and folk memories of conflict, as well as long centuries of interpenetration and coexistence. Islam was crucially important to the development of mediaeval Christian Europe, as a source of civilisation, as a challenge and as an antithesis against which Christendom defined itself.[3] The Crusades helped warp two civilisations; and Chechnya and Bosnia remind us that the same sort of religious and ethnic passions burn today. The interaction between the Moslem world and the West is the most vivid example against which to test Samuel Huntington's thesis that the clash of civilisations is becoming the decisive factor in the world's relationships.[4]

The situation in Palestine, our fourth issue, brings differences between the West and the Moslem world into sharp focus. Viewed narrowly, the Arab-Israel dispute contraposes only two parts of the Moslem and Western worlds: the Arabs of Palestine and their supporters throughout the Middle East, versus the Israeli people and their backers. Set in a historical context, it gives contemporary form to many of Islam's grievances: the burdening of the Arabs of Palestine with the consequences of a European genocide; Western neo-colonialism and the neglect of natural justice; and the demonisation of Arabs and Moslems.[5]

This point interacts with a fifth, otherwise separate issue: Moslem fundamentalism and the terrorism to which it sometimes leads. The sects of the American religious right, the Basque terrorists and the IRA, the Tamil Tigers and Hindu extremists, all demonstrate that fundamentalism and terrorism are not exclusively Moslem phenomena. Nevertheless, there are good reasons why the world is so conscious of Moslem fundamentalism and of terror that has roots within the Islamic world. It sees the extremes of fundamentalism in Afghanistan and Algeria. Religious and social practice in many less troubled Moslem states, such as Saudi Arabia and Pakistan, requires of the outside world an understanding which Islam does not always extend to others. And renegade states like Libya and Iran lend support to international terrorism.

The last issue brings matters home to Britain. Two million Moslems have put down roots here, erected 600 mosques. Increasingly, they see themselves not as immigrants but Britons, and among the younger generation at least the balance has tilted in that direction.[6] But the extent of their absorption into British life and retention of links elsewhere, their economic standing and their attitude to Islam as a religion, philosophy and social model all remain causes of discord within the Moslem community and, sometimes, with wider British society. Politically, their votes are a significant factor in a number of constituencies. A few of them are achieving great personal wealth and real economic weight. Others attract attention by the stridency of their religious and political views. This is Britain's largest and most significant minority.[7]

∿

Each of these issues involves British interests. Each needs separate analysis.

Islam is a global system of faith, philosophy and practice, but its adherents are predominantly concentrated in a belt that stretches halfway round the world from Indonesia, through Malaysia and the Indian subcontinent, into central Asia, the Middle East and Africa. It extends far beyond the Arab world, but has its origins and has its heart there.[8] Three of the world's ten most populous states – Indonesia, Pakistan and Bangladesh – are overwhelmingly Moslem. Four more – China, India, Russia and Nigeria – have large Moslem minorities. Most of these hundreds of millions demonstrate a religious conviction that other faiths have lost. In the last 20 years it has begun to take a more vigorous and articulate form, to the point where it is becoming a religious revival among one-fifth of the population of the earth. Islam is finding converts, particularly in Africa, while other faiths decline. Eight Arab countries have the fastest growing populations in the world. This is a system of thought and belief which reflects confidence about its future. It affects politics and economics as much as society and the private behaviour of the individual, for Islam does not make Christianity's distinction between God and Caesar: it assumes the right to opinions on worldly things which, to the more devout Moslems at least, have a religious authority.

The religious revival is making its mark on national politics. In some countries, as in Turkey, it is beginning to influence the attitudes of governments which are in principle resolutely secular. Elsewhere, as among the Taliban in Afghanistan, it is seizing power itself. In Algeria it wages civil war against governments. The revival is at its most dramatic where religious fundamentalism leads to extremist politics. But it is not an exclusively negative phenomenon, for at its best it gives Moslem societies behavioural benchmarks to set against materialism and ethical standards with which to combat corruption. The merits of this revival depend on the ends to which it turns and the means it uses.

It is possible that its architects could seize political command of broad areas of the Moslem world as they have in Iran. But it does not have the Islamic world to itself. There are profound differences within and between Islamic societies. Indonesia's role in the developing world goes back all the way to the enunciation of the five principles of non-alignment at Bandung in 1955.[9] Turkey has been a stalwartly secular member of NATO and is now a pressing applicant for European Union membership. Pakistan and Bangladesh present different versions of Islam in the subcontinent. In India one of the largest of all concentrations of Moslems forms a major part of a federal republic based on secular principles. Malaysia places less emphasis on acting as the spokesman for Islam than for the south-east Asian tigers. In much of the Middle East oil wealth is the most important formative influence upon society. Thus in most Moslem countries the faith's revival is shifting a political balance rather than seizing control.

In the past the British have claimed a particular understanding of large parts of the Moslem world. France met Islam in the Maghrib and Lebanon. Nineteenth-century Russian expansion took the tsar's troops into the Moslem Caucasus and central Asia. China has its Moslem provinces. But the British experience exceeded each of these in extent. In the subcontinent and the Sudan, in Malaya and Nigeria and the Arab world, the British traded, worked and soldiered with Moslem partners. They claimed a belief, real or assumed, in mutual trust between Christian and Moslem. They respected the dignity of Moslem princes, the hardness of Arab desert life. They considered the Mohammedan a worthy fighting man, whether among India's "martial races" or T E Lawrence's Arab allies. Other things brought a vulgarisation of the relationship, like the British soldier's mindless contempt for the Egyptian and parodies of little boys selling their scarcely larger sisters in the souk. But British scholars, administrators in the Sudan, political agents in the Gulf all claimed to understand and respect the Moslem world as the businessman does today.

The British still have some advantages in the eyes of many Moslems. The empire was both a negative and a positive influence; the Commonwealth is a marginal but positive one. In the Middle East, British administrators and diplomats won a blend of suspicion and respect. The Suez adventure in 1956 brought the extinction of Britain's power in the Arab world, yet it did not totally destroy its reputation for good judgment and understanding.[10] In Moslem eyes there is nothing as damaging in the British record as France's in Algeria, or the United States' uncritical support for Israel. So the British are somewhat better placed than their partners to position themselves favourably in the Moslem world.

They have a substantial stake in several countries. British companies have major interests in the oil of the Middle East, and are building them around the Caspian. Both areas, like Moslem south-east Asia, offer major opportunities for exports and investment. So do the subcontinent and Moslem northern Nigeria. Some of the countries of the Moslem swathe of the world could develop an economic significance comparable with those of the east Asian swathe which partly overlaps it. Their potential for Britain depends on their political stability; their economic dynamism; Britain's competitiveness in their markets; and their political and social attitudes towards Britain and the West. In the last chapter we looked at similar prospects in east Asia, and a later one explores the rest of the world. Are there special factors affecting such

Moslem economies?

Three question-marks stand out.They concern political stability, economic dynamism and the oil market. Politically the Moslem world has characteristics and contradictions of its own. Economically it has yet to demonstrate that Islam can bring it the success which in east Asia may be attributed to the influence of Confucius. But oil is an asset which offsets a multitude of weaknesses.

For around 50 years now many Moslem countries have been stretched on a rack of political differences. They have thrown off colonialism and most of the works of neo-colonialism. They have waged war: repeatedly with Israel, with Britain and France in 1956, with France in Algeria, with the Soviet Union in Afghanistan, and with India in Pakistan and Bangladesh. They have massacred half a million Chinese in Indonesia and come to uneasy terms with the Chinese in Malaysia. They have struggled with one another about the nature of their societies: monarchist or republican, tradition versus reform, fundamentalism versus modernity, almost always under authoritarian rather than democratic leadership. Their domestic travails have affected their external relationships, most particularly when religious fundamentalism has led (or has been seen as leading) to support for terror.

There is little evidence that the Moslem countries will become more democratic, more tolerant of dissent, or more open to Western opinion or advice. The outside world has little influence on them. For Britain the path of wisdom is good relations with incumbent governments, efforts to maximise their contacts with the outside world, the discreet promotion of respect for the opinions of others, together with a readiness to come to terms with change. Britain must take action when its economic or political interests are directly threatened by aggression. It must stand up for its own values against pressure even from its major markets. It must act against proven international terrorism. Beyond that there is little to be said for it trying to throw its weight around in regions from which its power receded the best part of half a century ago.[11]

The countries of the Islamic world are currently achieving very different standards of economic dynamism. Indonesia and Malaysia share in south-east Asia's boom. Some of the countries of the Middle East have oil wealth and the ability to build broader prosperity upon it.

Turkey has some of the qualities, such as national pride, personal discipline and a respect for education, on which economic achievement can be built. Of the rest, only Somalia, Afghanistan and Bangladesh are among the poorest of the poor. But taken as a whole the Moslem countries do not shine as models of the purposeful economic growth which in two decades can transform a society.

Business prospects for Britain in the Moslem world will therefore remain concentrated in south-east Asia and in the oil-rich countries of the Gulf and the Caspian: finding, developing and pumping oil, and servicing the demand for development which oil wealth generates. Thus the security of oil from the Gulf is a prime British interest. Other issues relate to it, such as the containment of Iraq, fundamentalism in Iran, exports and particularly arms exports. But oil is the chief reason for our interest in the Arab world. To care about its security is not, as critics argue, evidence of the cynicism and hypocrisy of western policy. We are right to want to defend a vital interest. We cannot separate that interest from the others which accrete to it.

The first priority is oil security itself. This required the vacation of Iraqi aggression against Kuwait and demands continuing political and if necessary military support for Saudi Arabia and the Gulf states. It could necessitate action to contain Iran. It brings other benefits as well as energy security: a Middle Eastern role in which Britain can cooperate whole-heartedly with the United States (as it should not, as is argued later, over Palestine), a reminder to our allies of the value of Britain's friendship and the preservation of important export markets. But its pursuit also imposes costs: the loss of life in the Gulf war, the cost of maintaining military capabilities with a long reach, and acquiescence in the actions of some less than savoury regional partners. Its biggest potential cost is being dragged into a continuing conflict between Arab traditionalists and radicals, with the danger that either or both will see the West's involvement as hostile to Islam. It is a risk that has to be taken, in the pursuit of high-priority benefits, but it fuels a suspicion that the West does indeed seek a conflict of civilisations with Islam. This concern is central to modern perceptions of the historical relationship between the Western and Moslem worlds.

That relationship involves over 1 billion Moslems on the one side, and something approaching that number of people on the other, whose civilisations look back to predominantly Christian origins. It goes back to the very early years of Islam, when it first burst out of Arabia while Christianity was still struggling to impose itself on Europe. It is also historically the best documented of all the interactions between major civilisations.

Norman Davies summarises the significance for European history of the first relationships between the Moslem world and Christendom.[12] The rise of Islam, which within two centuries of the Prophet's death in 632 had penetrated southern Europe, presented a challenge to Christendom when it was still vulnerable. At the same time it brought to it much of the culture on which its mediaeval flowering would be based. The relationship was therefore at once antagonistic, with the Moslem conquest of Spain and penetration into France, and symbiotic, with Islamic scholarship providing for example the essential links between Aristotle and Aquinas. Christians hated, feared, respected and learned from Moslems. So Islam contributed both as a challenge and a source of inspiration to Christendom's own sense of identity. And Islam, expanding not just westwards against Europe but eastwards against marauders in Asia, provided a kind of protective cradle around Christendom.

The Crusades altered the nature of the relationship.[13] Christendom pressed upon Asia as Islam had pressed upon Europe and brought a new viciousness to the conflict. For 200 years wars, raids and sieges heightened the sense of challenge to both faiths in their struggles in the Near East; and in Spain Christian campaigning against Moslem continued for two centuries longer. Antipathy for the other overlaid the original symbiosis between faiths and came to characterise the faiths themselves. Crusader castles in the Levant, uncertainly sustained by the prayers and money of Christendom, typified a "sense of siege" between the faiths that has persisted into our own times.[14]

Even when the physical conflict was over and Christendom had been expelled from the Holy Land and Islam at last from the Kingdom of Granada, the two civilisations developed on antipathetic lines, their relationships with one another conducted less by scholars and statesmen than by the slave traders of the Mediterranean.[15] Christendom expanded aggressively into the world, building material success that was expressed in European empires and the worldly triumph of European ideas. Islam by comparison faded, its early intellectual and ethical achievements appropriated by others. Now, when the supremacy of European material achievements is being challenged at last, it is not Islam but the disciples of Confucius who lay the strongest claim to take the West's place. For Islam's religious revival is not as yet paralleled by material success. "Moslems, almost without exception, feel a sense of shame and humiliation at the submergence of a once proud Islamic culture. Many resent a world order which seems to entrench Western political and cultural dominance." [16]

Attitudes on what was once the Christian side of the divide are sometimes paranoid also. In Russia suspicions of gangsters from the southern republics of the old Soviet Union are as concerned with ethnic difference as with criminality. The face of French society is disfigured by hostility to its large Moslem minority. Britain has its share of suspicions of Islam: liberal suspicion of the condemnation of Salman Rushdie or of Islam's attitudes to women, as much as vulgar suspicion of the seemingly suspect ways of the working-class Moslem minority in the back streets of Birmingham and Bradford.

It is a recurring theme of this book that emotion plays as large a part as reason in shaping British attitudes to the rest of the world; this is certainly the case where attitudes to Islam are concerned. There is no magic wand solution to the problem, but there are ways to minimise it. The first is to build on Britain's strong academic and practical knowledge of the Moslem world, and propagate in wider circles a better understanding of the underlying doctrines and practice of Islam. The work for inter-faith understanding of people such as the Prince of Wales and Prince Hassan of Jordan is a good example here. A second is to try to see Moslem fundamentalism and terrorism in proportion and in context, recognising, for example, the links between the Lockerbie atrocity and the shooting down by the United States Navy of an Iranian airliner over the Gulf six months earlier. A third way is to build up a wider range of contacts with the countries of the Moslem world, even when mutual suspicion make it difficult to take the process far beyond the official and the businesslike. It is important to subject attempts to isolate pariah Moslem states to rigorous critical assessment:

when the nations have finished punishing Iran for its death sentence on Salman Rushdie or Libya for its support of terrorism, they will still remain actors on the world scene, probably made the more recalcitrant by attempts to isolate them. In all this work there is a particular role for the British. They know the Moslem world better than most of their partners, and they are less threatened than some of them by the excesses of its fanatics.

$$\backsim$$

Among all the occasions of incomprehension between Islam and the West the most pressing and immediate is the Arab-Israel dispute. The problem of Palestine is the issue which above all others sets large parts of the Moslem world against the West and in which Moslems detect the most extreme form of western prejudice. They see it as an issue which engages the faith and credit of the West, which has been created not by a conflict between western and Islamic worlds but by the West's own prejudices and politics. Rome destroyed the Jewish kingdom of Palestine; Christianity created the anti-Semitism which Europeans directed at Jews; European fascism destroyed the Jewish people; western guilt created Israel by way of compensation; and the needs of American domestic politics sustain an expansionist Israel with no interest in even-handed accommodation with its neighbours and with the Arabs of Israel.[17]

One does not have to be a Zionist to question parts of that perception of the Palestine dispute. But one does not have to be an Arab to see the force of much of it. Forget the story of how the Arab-Israel dispute arose. Discount for the moment both the West's need for Arab oil and its sense of obligation to an Israel which grew out of a great European crime. Look at the situation in Israel, the occupied territories and Lebanon today and you see, if you are dispassionate, a situation in which the West as a whole and the United States in particular do less than justice to the Arab case and more than justice to Israel's. In the Lebanon, Israel and its proxies pursue illegal and violent policies, often in defiance of the United Nations. Around Jerusalem the extremists of the Israeli right, many of them of United States origin, set themselves to force the Palestinians out or to provoke them to violence which will destroy the peace process. The present Israeli government tries to shift on to Palestinian shoulders the responsibility for crushing the terrorists whom its own policies provoke. And the attitudes of many Israelis to their Arab neighbours have passed beyond an understandable antagonism to crude racism. Today's Israel is not a society with which objective Westerners can honourably identify.

The situation in Palestine is not one in which Britain today can exercise much influence. Balfour licensed the creation of the Jewish national home in Palestine but our direct power vanished from the territory in 1947, and much of our influence in 1956.[18] Today the only outside power with decisive clout in the area is the United States and its policies towards it are fatally skewed. But the European Union has some influence there, however much it may be resented by the United States and Israel, and within the European Union Britain retains a particular authority on the subject. We have reasons of our own to make a stand, for the dispute damages British interests directly through its impact on our relations with the oil-producing Arab countries in particular, and through the impression it makes on the minds of the Moslem world. It is an issue on which Britain, in European company, can distance itself from the prejudice and unfairness which even moderate Moslem opinion detects in uncritical American support for Israel. There is no reason to let Israeli sensitivities and American prejudices deter us from taking a position of our own, in favour of the creation of a Palestine state. The objective facts of the situation require that we should do so. So does the broader necessity of trying to find common ground with the Moslem world on the wide range of issues on which we come together. The safety of Israel is a legitimate Western goal in Middle East politics. The expansion of Israel and its pursuit of a spurious security through pre-eminence in the area is not.[19]

⌒

To many Britons fundamentalism and terrorism seem to be central and linked characteristics of the world of contemporary Islam. But the two phenomena need to be looked at on their own, set in context, as far as possible explained, and related to British interests and concerns. Both are slippery concepts.

My dictionary defines fundamentalism as "strict adherence to traditional orthodox tenets (e.g. the literal inerrancy of Scripture) held to be fundamental to the Christian faith: opposed to *liberalism* and *modernism*" (italics in the original). Such strict adherence to Christian faith persists today, even in sceptical, practical Britain. Elsewhere it flourishes, as for example in many parts of the United States. Similar fundamentalism is to be found in other societies and other faiths. But the stridency of some Moslem fundamentalist teachers and the willingness of some Moslem societies to follow them attract particular attention. Nevertheless, fundamentalists remain minorities among the complexities of the huge Islamic world.

In western eyes, aspects of Moslem fundamentalism may seem absurd and threatening. But a century ago Protestants levelled such charges against Roman Catholicism. Today the secular West extends a careful courtesy to most forms of religious belief, to Catholicism, Jewry, Protestant fundamentalism and the less demanding Christian faiths, but often denies it to the Moslem variety of fundamentalism. Yet it deserves as much respect as the strict interpretations of other faiths which also may seem wrong-headed to those who do not share them.

Terrorism preoccupies the whole world and is in principle a quite separate issue from fundamentalism. But some terrorism is based in Moslem states and concerned with issues that affect the Islamic world; and some of that Moslem part of the world's terrorism flows from the urgent requirements of fundamentalism. In Felipe Fernandez-Armesto's words, " Militancy and violence are as different from one another as bark from bite".[20] But unfortunately circumstances provide some justification for the world's tendency to confuse them.

The fight against international terrorism necessarily transcends frontiers, but different countries bring different characteristics to it. Britain brings two approaches, complementary or contradictory as you care to see them, in an unusually heightened form. One the one hand, it is among the foremost in its resistance to terrorism. Our police and special forces have developed a particular expertise in fighting terrorism; successive governments have been unusually outspoken on the need not to bargain with terrorists (such as hostage-takers) or with those (such as Sinn Fein) whose politics are interwoven with violence. Britain can lay some claim to being terrorism's most implacable opponent. On the other hand, British negotiators have time and again come to terms with those whose political arguments are reinforced by violence, as in the process of decolonisation and in Northern Ireland today. For experience has taught us that democracies have little chance of inflicting military defeat on terrorists who believe they have real grievances and who fight for substantial change. Today both the IRA and Moslem terrorism claim precisely these grievances and the necessity to fight for change. Despite setbacks, Britain remains committed to the search for a political solution in Northern Ireland. Although it does not have similar direct responsibility in the Middle East, it should follow the same instincts about Moslem terrorism, seeking to understand its causes and find political ways to remove them.

⌐

The substantial Moslem minority in Britain presents a very different face of Islam. It has its extravagant spokesmen, but Britain's 2 million Moslems are mostly moderate and disproportionately young, and well over half of them were born in Britain. It is a community whose members increasingly think of themselves as Britons, but with a strong sense of its own religious and ethnic cohesion. With its continuing links with the subcontinent, it presents a classic example of the "multiple" or "layered" identities examined in Chapter 1.

Any ethnically distinct minority encounters substantial difficulties with the majority in today's Britain. It faces problems in securing self-evident rights, such as everyday security for its members, equal treatment before the law and good relations with its neighbours. The position of the Moslem minority, however, seems less explosive than that of the Afro-Caribbean. Its problems are more ones of withdrawal and isolation from the majority than of confrontation with it. It experiences, nevertheless, substantial prejudice, whose root causes are vulgar xenophobia and racism, but which feeds on some aspects of Moslem practice, such as the frequent subservience and isolation of the female. But the existence of this minority has a formative influence on British attitudes towards the outside world, and in particular towards the Islamic countries. It brings the issues of Britain's relationships with a great system of thought and belief, and with a part of the world of increasing importance, home to our own corner shops.[21]

❧

Let us try to summarise where Britain stands in relation to the Islamic world. We form a part of the Western community of nations which is intimately and sometimes antagonistically connected with that huge proportion of humanity. But we have our own distinct position within the western camp. We are less dependent than Japan and continental Europe on Gulf oil. We are less exposed than Mediterranean Europe to the pressures of Moslem immigration. Uncritical American hostility to Israel's enemies has no parallel here. We have better facilities than many western countries for bridge-building with the Moslem world.

Nevertheless, we cannot detach ourselves from the West's desire to protect its own interests while improving relations with the Moslem world. We need the global political and commercial stability which the loss of Gulf oil would undermine. We want access to Middle Eastern markets. Our political and military capacity in the Moslem world is something which our partners value. NATO and European Union memberships bind us to partners confronted with problems arising from Moslem sources more acute than those we face. We can influence western attitudes towards the Moslem world and so begin to eat away at causes of conflict and misunderstanding. To do so can help to modify Moslem attitudes also. We should start within our own hearts and minds, too many of them infected with instinctive prejudice against some manifestations of Islam.

As we examine our consciences we must distinguish between the religious faith and practice of hundreds of millions; the political superstructure which some hundreds of thousands may build upon it; and the violent expression of Moslem political or religious conviction practised by a few thousand extremist political and religious leaders. Political interest and lazy analysis may confuse the three; but these are distinct phenomena, calling for distinct responses. The first deserves respect, however unfamiliar its forms. The second calls for a sustained effort to understand it and come to terms with it. The third needs a precision of response that the West has so far not achieved: exact political and security intelligence followed by a measured legal and security response that is demonstrably appropriate and justifiable.

Britain must not forget that the West's relationship with the Moslem world is genuinely as much symbiotic as antagonistic. The present-day Moslem world cannot live without the West. The West cannot live without Islam. Britain, knowing the Moslem world better than its neighbours and with a historical reputation for influence in many parts of it, can promote understanding between the two. Its aim must be to diminish what is hostile in the relationship and increase each side's understanding and acceptance of the other.

1   Malise Ruthven, *Islam in the World* (Harmondsworth: Penguin, 1991).

2   See BP, *Statistical Review of World Energy*, 1997.

3   Norman Davies, *Europe: A History* (Oxford: Oxford University Press, 1991).

4   Samuel P Huntington, first propounded in *Foreign Affairs,* Summer 1993, as "The Clash of Civilizations?", and developed, without the question-mark, in *The Clash of Civilizations and the Remaking of World Order* (New York: Simon & Schuster, 1996).

5   Ian J Bickerton and Carla L Klausner, *A Concise History of the Arab-Israeli Conflict* (Englewood: Prentice Hall, 1995).

6   For convincing fictional portrayals of the process see the work of Hanif Kureishi, and particularly *The Black Album* (London: Faber and Faber 1995).

7   Philip Lewis, *Islamic Britain: Religion, Politics and Identity among British Moslems* (London: I B Tauris, 1994).

8   Albert Hourani, *A History of the Arab Peoples* (London: Faber & Faber, 1991).

9   National independence, sovereignty, equality, territorial inviolability and self-determination, as propounded by Third World leaders meeting in Bandung, Indonesia, in 1955.

10 Keith Kyle, *Suez* (London: Weidenfeld & Nicolson, 1991).

11 See Alan Munro, "Entente Islamique" in *Prospect*, August/September 1996, and subsequent correspondence with Josef Joffe.

12 Norman Davies, *op. cit.*

13 Steven Runciman, *History of the Crusades* (Cambridge: Cambridge University Press, 1951).

14 Graham E Fuller and Ian O Lesser, *A Sense of Siege: Geopolitics of Islam and the West* (Oxford: Oxford University Press, 1995).

15 Fernand Braudel, *The Mediterranean and the Mediterranean World in the Age of Philip II* (New York: Harper & Row, 1972).

16 "Islam and the West", unpublished Foreign & Commonwealth Office conference paper.
17 Dilip Hiro, *Sharing the Promised Land: An Interwoven Tale of Israelis and Palestinians* (London: Hodder & Stoughton, 1996).
18 Christopher Sykes, *Cross Roads to Israel* (London: Collins, 1965).
19 See the Runnymede Trust's report, *Islamophobia: a challenge for us all* (London: Runnymede Trust, 1997).
20 Felipe Fernandez-Armesto, *Millennium* (London: Bantam Press, 1995).
21 Yezid Sayigh, *Armed Struggle and the Search for State* (Oxford: Oxford University Press, 1997).

10   Picking up the Kremlin's pieces

For more than half a century the Soviet Union had a central place in the British people's view of the world. In the war we put our faith in the Red Army, and told ourselves many comforting lies about the nature of our Soviet ally. We hoped that after the war the Soviet Union would join its allies in a system of order that would give the United Nations effective teeth.

Then, as the Kremlin began to unveil postwar intentions that had little in common with our own, our perceptions of the Soviet Union changed, but not the importance we accorded to it. We watched the Communist takeover of power in eastern Europe. We feared the accumulation of Soviet military might in East Germany. Soviet propaganda sought to exploit our difficulties as we shed the empire, and we fought Soviet influence round the world in an east-west contest for the hearts and minds of the developing world. A sense of the evil of Moscow Centre and the Gulag seeped into our literary consciousness from the pages of Le Carré and Solzhenitsyn. The ideology of Marxism presented the main intellectual challenge to our own philosophies. For more than 40 years, throughout a period in which we defined our place in the world largely in terms of the Atlantic Alliance, the Soviet Union was our cold war foe and our potential enemy.

Britain's response to that threat shaped its view of itself and many of its institutions. It buttressed our belief in ourselves as the United States' most reliable ally. The Soviet challenge turned the British army into a tank army, committed to the defence of northern Germany. Out of it came the RAF's low-level, airfield-busting tactics, first encountering real anti-aircraft fire in Operation Desert Storm, and the Royal Navy's preoccupation with the North Atlantic and the Arctic. Possession of an independent deterrent, its use imaginable only in response to Soviet attack, was a prime component of British defence policy, which stretched budgets, divided moralists and enraged activists opposed to it. Generations of British diplomats matured as advocates of alliance in confrontation with the Soviet Union and as analysts of the Soviet threat: not just as Kremlinologists but as global practitioners for whom, in every situation and negotiation, the Soviet Union was the ultimate opponent and the KGB man the figure behind the arras.[1]

In 1989 came the year of miracles. That it ended happily was due above all to Soviet self-restraint. This changed Western perceptions of Soviet policy; and as the countries of central and eastern Europe recovered their freedom and the Soviet political and military presence in central Europe vanished down the memory hole, a chief preoccupation of British policy was removed. Then, in the wake of the abortive coup of 1991, the Soviet Union and Communism themselves evaporated. The Soviet empire in eastern Europe had been dismantled with less loss of life than any other, and the continent of a country stretching between the Gulf of Finland and the Bering Straits lost its sinister salience.[2]

But its importance persisted, and this was an importance of weakness as much as of strength. Whereas in the past the Kremlin's intentions had been veiled by authoritarian secrecy, now they were developed in semi-public, with all the changeability of a society in which many struggled for power and few knew exactly what they wanted to do with it. Moscow remained as difficult to read as ever. It now posed a low level of direct threat to the West's interests, but at the same time it offered a low level of stability and predictability.

～

Between 1989 and 1991 the Soviet Union entered a period of change as fundamental as that which racked Russia between 1917 and 1921. It is not over yet, and Russia continues to confront the world with profound uncertainties. As authority and ideology both fell away, Russians became free to express themselves as they had not been since 1920. All the characteristics of a great nation and a tapestry of populations were released from Communist orthodoxy and revealed in their contradictory complexity. Russia's diversity and perversity, the personal dignity, ingenuity and initiative of the individual Russian, the enterprise, sloth, energy and corruption of ordinary Russians, all emerged from behind the curtain of Communist uniformity. Any nation has its share of such contradictions; Tolstoy, Dostoevsky and Turgenev suggest that they were present in unusual intensity in historic Russia, and Gogol adds to the picture a specifically Russian celebration of the absurd; under Communism contradictions simmered, the more intense because frustrated and little expressed, for 70 years. Now they are once again in free play, to confuse anyone, Russian or outsider, who seeks to establish where Russia is heading today, nearly ten years after the year of miracles.[3]

Its new destiny is shaped by many influences. The search for something better than the old Soviet order has produced democracy of a kind, with reasonably honest free elections. There is an uncertain awareness of the need for accountability to parliament, the media, the general public, the electorate. The idea of an open, dispassionate legal system is putting down shallow roots. So is belief in human and individual rights. So are a few of the institutions of a civil society. All these concepts, unknown in the Soviet Union and largely alien to historic Russia also, have their Russian believers and advocates. Some of them are opportunists, some idealists, people who are prepared, as they showed in resisting the 1991 coup, to die to preserve these advances. They are giving these foreign concepts specifically Russian interpretations.[4]

Beside them are the concepts of economic reform, which give Russian citizens a chance to earn a living or create a fortune and which are endowing the country with the beginnings of business enterprise, meaningful markets, comprehensible prices and the framework of a capitalist economy. These too have their advocates and disciples, coming from every background and none, with a mixture again of opportunists and idealists. They want to make Russia economically efficient and to enrich themselves. Like the advocates of political reform, they look more likely than not to prevail. Inflation, which in 1992 seemed to be spiralling out of control, has been reined in. Fiscal policy is tight

143

enough to win continuing IMF support. Investment, overwhelmingly Russian rather than foreign, is being poured into new companies and into new firms spun off from the old state-owned monoliths. By the middle of 1994, 80 per cent of Russia's industrial companies had been privatised, and 70 per cent of the country's GDP is now generated by the private sector. That sector today is vibrant, even frenetic; and it is becoming crudely effective. Most Russians may still be learning the most elementary lessons of ordinary commercial life as the West understands it, but some have learned fast and have already reaped the benefits of wealth and power. They occupy every sector of economic enterprise: as bankers, importers, exporters, economic analysts, insurers, retailers and industrialists. All cry out in their different ways for a more reliable commercial infrastructure: business-friendly economic policies, knowable commercial law, predictable taxation and reliable communications.[5]

Against these political and economic innovators are ranged those who hanker after the certainties and the opportunities of the old order, the people who gave Zyuganov 40 per cent of the vote in the 1996 presidential elections. They include Communist old believers, military men and security men deprived of their old power and position, the poor, pensioners, the dispossessed and some of the old captains of Soviet industry. They want very different things, ranging from stable prices to preserve the value of their pitiful pensions, to a reassertion of military power and glory as a great nation, even an imperial nation. They preach populism and nationalism and can bring demonstrators into the streets. But they bear many of the marks of losers, of people left behind by history. In today's Russia there can be no absolute assurance that nostalgia such as theirs will remain permanently excluded from power, but the odds are that it will.[6]

There are other influences which abuse the new system. The border between business and commercial crime is little understood and ill policed. Taxes are resented and avoided. Billions of dollars find offshore homes. Corruption distorts business and buys economic and political favour. Violence stalks business, and crime is a commonplace way to obtain, buttress and exploit political power. It is impossible to assess the real power of all these interests. But every anecdote suggests that they are very strong and they may be on the way to consuming the state.

Criminal conspiracies may even have pulled off the crime of the century, "the theft of the Second Russian Revolution".[7]

So Russia's future is in dispute between reformers, reactionaries and criminals. The outcome could produce any one of a range of different Russian futures. At worst, the result could be a country lost to criminality and corruption, its politicians no more than front men for villains, its economics distorted by the power of corrupt interests, its streets patrolled by the security forces of authoritarian rulers or fought over by the private armies of criminal interests. Such a state could fall victim to secession, civil war and anarchy.

Another scenario would give back to Russia something of its authoritarian, superficially orderly past under the leadership of scarcely reconstructed Communists or of a strong man. Such a Russia would deal harshly with some aspects of the criminality which threatens to consume the state but incorporate others into the state system. It might continue some of the political and economic advances of the last seven years, or it might revert to the deadly inanition of the fading years of Soviet rule. It could concern itself almost exclusively with the country's domestic problems or begin to pose a threat to its neighbours in its "near abroad" and in eastern Europe once again.

Neither of these scenarios offers the majority of Russians much prospect of freedom, stability and prosperity. The criminal option could take the country into something like the organised corruption of today's Nigeria, with wealth concentrated in the hands of the few. The reactionary option would provide stability, at the price of Russia's recent hard-won freedoms, and the hope of modest prosperity, making of Russia a less successful imitation of some of the authoritarian countries of Asia and Latin America.

A third scenario sees the continuance of the uneasy progress towards political pluralism and economic liberalism which Russia has made in the 1990s. Most of Russia's historical experience argues against it but on today's evidence this seems the most likely of these three scenarios. And if Russia can achieve it, it could astonish the world by achieving in the first quarter of the 21st century something of what the United States achieved in the second half of the 19th. If Russia can recover its morale and retain its ordinary peoples' capacity for self-sacrifice, it could use its human capital, space and raw materials to create a modern, continental-sized state of new openness and opportunity. For critical as its position is today, it is perhaps less critical than that of China in the Cultural Revolution. It has real assets: the greatest reserves of minerals and energy in the world, a well-educated and above all a scientifically educated work force, and a powerful sense of national identity. In Russia today enormous promise competes for attention with present problems. Its economy could become the world's next major miracle, with growth of anything from 5 per cent to 10 per cent per year sustained for decades. Such growth would suck in outside investment, accelerating progress still further: investment in the exploitation of the country's raw materials, in building an infrastructure that truly binds society together and in providing the consumer goods and services for which ordinary Russians have waited for so long.[8]

Whichever course Russia takes, it will continue to matter to the world. It numbers 150 million people, educated, ingenious and tenacious. It has nearly twice the space of the United States, extending across 11 of the world's time zones. It has the skills and raw materials to grow out of the black hole into which the old Soviet system fell. It has lost the Soviet Union's superpower status but it retains its nuclear weapons and a special relationship of a kind with the United States. The country turns its eastern face to the new Asian and Pacific centres of economic gravity, with a long frontier with China and an exposure to the Pacific and the Sea of Japan. Its southern republics involve it with all the problems and possibilities of the Islamic world. In Europe, Russia still looms over Ukraine and the Baltic states and less immediately over the countries of eastern and central Europe; and it looks with reciprocated suspicion at the federation or confederation which it sees forming around its historic enemy, Germany. Even a broken Russia would have much to say for itself. An authoritarian Russia could once again threaten its neighbours; so could an economically successful one, using economic power for hostile political purposes; or it could involve them more constructively as active partners in its development. Like China today, it could threaten with stick and tempt with carrot simultaneously.

Britain has a clear interest in the emergence of a Russia which is at peace with itself, increasingly prosperous and above all predictable. The third of our scenarios offers a chance of achieving it. The Russians themselves will make all the main decisions about their future with little input from outsiders. But foreigners have some influence in Russia and some opportunities to affect developments there. Let us look at where the British stand among these foreign influences, starting with the historical relationship between the two countries.

The British and the Russians have been conscious of one another for centuries, more often than not uneasily, with the British usually taking a censorious view of Russia. To the Elizabethans, Russia was a remote and barbarous kingdom, but one rich in trading promise. In the eyes of 18th-century Britons it was an empire torn between its ancient ways and its modernising ambitions. The defeat of Napoleon brought it into Europe, where it took its place among the victorious allies at the Congress of Vienna, and it held that place throughout the 19th century. But to the parliamentary and increasingly democratic British it remained an arbitrary empire, an enemy in the Crimean War and a threat – imaginary or real – to India. The horrors of the Russian Revolution brought a changed perspective but left intact the old reserve in British attitudes towards Russia. That reserve was broken by a few short years of British worship of Soviet heroism in the Second World War; but in the 40 years that followed it the British, standing up to be counted beside the United States, took an even harsher view than other western Europeans of the brutality of Soviet policy within the Communist world, and of the threat that Moscow posed outside it.

Russian views of Britain present a mirror image of British views of Russia. On the foundations of Peter the Great's interest in the British as shipbuilders and seafarers grew up an interest in them as merchants, parliamentarians and industrialists. But it was an interest of dissimilars: the interest of a land empire in a maritime one, of an autocracy in a parliamentary system, and of an essentially rustic society in the world's first industrial workshop. In consequence, reserve permeated this interest; and this reserve persisted into the 20th century, even when the occasions for it were reversed. So the Bolshevik regicides observed the world's principal surviving monarchy. The revolutionary Soviet society looked at Britain's traditional one. And after the period of limited sense of togetherness generated by wartime alliance, the Soviet Union reciprocated Britain's particular cold-war animosity, seeing the British as the closest supporter of the United States and the last serious imperialists.

So there is a historical distance between Britons and Russians today. They share also a sense of geographical distance: not just the miles that separate them but the different attitudes which differing geographies have given them. One cherishes insularity, looking to the sea as moat, while the other has always believed itself exposed to hostile neighbours, its security lying in its own spaces and in expansion. But Britain and Russia have some important things in common too. Each thinks of itself as a serious, historic nation. Each cherishes victory in the Second World War over a Germany about which each still retains its reservations. Permanent membership of the Security Council is a badge of distinction to both. So is the possession of nuclear weapons. Above all, neither country is sure about its relationship with the rest of Europe.

Most of these shared characteristics are nostalgic or negative. There is little material here on which to build policies in common for the future. Britain is inside the European Union: its debate with itself is essentially about whether it is happy there. Russia is outside, and going to remain so: its debate is about how to come to terms with that reality. The two countries share a concern with NATO, but one looks at it, from inside, as essential to Europe's security, the other, from outside, as an encroaching danger to its own well-being. Nevertheless, each country has reason to take the other seriously, and Russia is a factor which Britain must take into account in deciding where it belongs in the world.

It has to consider in the first place whether the western approach to change within Russia is on the right lines; and where it should put its weight within western debate on the subject. Since 1989 it has used its voice in NATO, the European Union, the World Bank, the IMF, the European Bank for Reconstruction and Development and the Organisation for Security and Co-operation in Europe to argue for selective intervention. The British spoke with the majority in opposing the romantically impracticable ideas of a Marshall Plan for the Soviet Union but did their best to promote the more down-to-earth proposal of a stabilisation fund for the rouble. In its own assistance to Russia, the

British government has put most emphasis on precisely targeted small schemes to underpin political and economic reform, and through them has made a useful if small contribution to Russian recovery. It has also lent encouragement to private voluntary and non-government initiatives which emerged after 1989. British banks have been active in Russia and some of the southern republics, and so has British industry.

But Britain's efforts, like those of all outsiders, have made only a slight difference to developments, and it has had less impact than some of its partners. Its political influence has been slight by comparison with that of the United States, as has its economic influence by comparison with that of Germany. (It is symptomatic, for example, that nowhere in the indexes of two important books on today's Russia appear the words "Britain", "British" or "United Kingdom".)[9] What influence it has exerted has mostly been through international and European interventions, whose achievements – if marginal – have on the whole been beneficial.

Russia, however, poses for Britain more fundamental political questions than how to make a marginal contribution to its political and economic rebirth. The most serious is security, in two distinct forms. One is security in the formal, traditional sense: security against menace or attack by a country which retains formidable, if run-down, military capacity and whose unpredictability makes impossible to rule out an attempt one day to use its power outside its borders. The other is security against the fall-out from the collapse of the Soviet Union: the proliferation of nuclear and other weapons, whether by the Russian state or by criminals and mavericks; the nations and private terrorists into whose hands such weapons might fall; the environmental menace of decaying weapons systems; and the international crime that a frustrated Russia is already fostering. Both threats demand a collaborative, integrated western effort to confront them.

The traditional security threat is at present low. Nuclear capacity apart, Russian forces have lost most of their ability to project significant power abroad. But a Russia emerging from its present weakness could rebuild and reshape them, so that in the first decades of the next century they could again present a challenge to the West. NATO is militarily diminished since its cold-war heyday, but it retains the most formidable integrated war-fighting capacity in the world. It assures the defence of western Europe. It locks the United States into a vital relationship with Europe. It remains an essential element in the political stability of the Atlantic and European worlds and essential insurance against threatening change in Russia. Earlier chapters have argued for Britain in Europe taking a more assertive and if necessary distanced attitude towards the United States. The potential security threat from a reviving and expanding Russia reminds us of the need to ensure that such shifts do not reduce the essential cohesion of NATO.

Britain's nuclear capacity is a significant element in the Atlantic defensive and deterrent system. Many argue that with the collapse of the Soviet Union and the Warsaw Pact it has lost its last justification. Against that, although Russia's defence spending is currently running at a level below that of Britain, it is still building nuclear submarines and investing in advanced strike aircraft. The United States is a less predictable ally than it was: it is a bold man who is entirely confident that American forces will still be in Europe 25 years from now. So in the next century western Europeans could find themselves without the United States and facing a resurgent Russia possessing nuclear weapons. France is not a reliable counterweight to Russia in the European nuclear balance. So long term prudence comes down heavily in favour of retaining some British nuclear capacity, beside closer cooperation within the Western European Union and continuing worldwide efforts to fight the dissemination of and reduce global levels of nuclear armaments.

The existing Atlantic Alliance is no threat to Russia, as moderate Russian opinion recognises. Its expansion eastwards is a different matter, bringing into conflict at least three legitimate concerns. The first is the need of the central and east Europeans for institutional guarantees of their security and independence. The second is the organisation's right to bring in any country which fulfils its requirements. The third, quite as legitimate as the other two when seen from Moscow, is Russia's historic concern about exclusion from, access to and defence against the West. For the time being, the deed is done, since NATO is committed to extending membership to Poland, the Czech Republic and Hungary. A second extension of NATO could bring in members, such as the three Baltic states, which are very much more controversial in Russian eyes. Wherever the eastward extension of NATO stops there will be those who, willingly or otherwise, remain outside it. There will remain the task of bringing them reassurance and of soothing the Kremlin's susceptibilities.

That task is one in the first place for the Atlantic Alliance itself, in integrating the new members and building a reassuring relationship with those outside. For some, such as the Baltic states, which still fear Russia but cannot be brought within NATO, European Union membership can provide implicit if not express security. For Russia, and for others who feel themselves threatened by NATO enlargement, the way ahead is to help them build relationships of confidence with NATO, without giving them a *droit de regard* over its policies. For all there is also a continuing role for the Organisation for Security and Co-operation in Europe: not to replace the Atlantic Alliance, but to extend the balm of cooperation and understanding as the CSCE did with such unexpected success in the closing years of the cold war.[10]

Any specifically British role in all this is limited; but there are things Britain is particularly well qualified to do. First, Russia and the central and eastern Europeans take it seriously as a military power. To their eyes, the Falklands campaign was as quixotically impressive as the Charge of the Light Brigade, with a more successful outcome. They recognise it as one of NATO's leading European members, with a strong voice in its political and security counsels. Second, it presents no threat, historical or contemporary, to anyone in central and eastern Europe and the former Soviet Union. Third, it has friends and contacts throughout central and eastern Europe. There is a place in the area for a second western European nation besides Germany. For Germany's strengths – its historic connections and its political and economic efforts today – are also weaknesses, constantly recalling what a less benign Germany has done in that part of the world over the centuries.[11]

The other, new security problem flows from Russia's inability to sustain the military machine that it created in its years as a superpower. In so far as Russia as a state seeks to export dangerous weapons to dangerous destinations, the cure is a matter of careful, carrot-and-stick diplomacy. In so far as individuals, private organisations, the mafia itself pursue this dangerous game, the response requires tireless supervision, the work of inspectors, secret services, customs officers and policemen. The post-Soviet element is a critically important part of the range of non-traditional security problems to be considered in Chapter 12. Here once again the familiar refrain emerges: these are problems in which the world has moved beyond the range of any single national actor and has to look to painstaking measures taken by international organisations or by nations working together, to international cooperation as intimate as that between separate agencies of national governments only a generation ago.[12]

Russia's economic and business relationships with Britain and the rest of the world are as important as its political ones. It will be an increasingly significant source of raw materials, all the way from Siberian gold and gas to the oil of the southern republics. A flourishing Russia will have an insatiable appetite for Western imports and investment. Recovering Russian industry will go looking for the foreign markets it has lost, particularly in central Europe and the developing countries. Thus much outside assistance to Russia serves the express purpose not just of strengthening Russia's political, economic and business prospects, but also of improving the donors' and lenders' positioning so as to share the benefits of Russia's recovery when it comes.

Britain is not well placed to win a major share in these benefits. In the old days, only Germany rivalled the east European countries as an exporter to the Soviet Union. It still has the lion's share of the Russian market for western imports, just as it has provided the bulk of western direct investment. Britain can point to its substantial imports from Russia, to individual British investments in industrial capacity there and, more significantly, to a strong position in the energy sector both in Russia itself and in the southern republics. But whatever happens to the Russian market, it is difficult to see Britain coming better than a poor seventh or eighth in the western race to serve it.

But it has every opportunity to play a full part in a relationship of growing importance between the European Union and Russia. That relationship is going to be composed of love and hate in the usual fluctuating proportions, but it cannot fail to be a significant one, since Russia cannot escape the importance of the European Union's role as the central element of organisation for western Europe today and for central and eastern Europe by the early years of the next century.

This political and economic reality has the economic and commercial muscle to help Russia today and make it a good partner tomorrow. Russia has a big interest in the Union's capacity to help to deliver a "European Germany" rather than a "German Europe". But its expansion into eastern Europe will present a continuing hurt to Russia's pride. Thinking Russians may recognise that their country is just too big to be included in a Union which it would overwhelm. But the European Union is set on a course of eastward expansion. It will include parts of Russia's "near abroad" before long. The Russian psyche will find it hard to accept a new division of Europe which suggests that Russia is not really a European state.[13] How these psychological problems are resolved depends on how Russia and its immediate neighbours develop internally over the years ahead. But whatever the nature of its society tomorrow, Russia is likely to go on pressing the European Union for a privileged relationship, and in particular for privileged access to its central and east European member states. It is a recipe for trade policy friction between Moscow and Brussels quite as irritating as that between Brussels and Washington today.

Russia's second response to continuing exclusion from an expanding European Union is likely to be to attempt to build a comparable organisation in the former Soviet Union. It has already rebuilt something of what was lost when the members of the Commonwealth of Independent States tried to go their own way. It could start to build on what are still uneasy and profoundly unequal relationships something more intimate, more committed and more operationally significant. Such a grouping might strengthen Russia's chances of building a strong economy on a wider basis. It might improve its chances of benefiting from the exploitation of the energy assets of the southern republics, which would increase its attractions to outsiders as a place to invest and sell in and to buy from. Conversely, it might involve Russia in political, post-colonial entanglements, as in Chechnya, that sapped its energies and damaged its reputation for respect for democracy and human rights. Above all, it might give Russia a counterweight to the European

Union, and comfort for its exclusion from it. The Western and the British interest is to see Russia draw what strength and solace it can from a regional grouping to match the European Union without regaining imperial rights in its "near abroad".

∽

When we try to decide where Russia is going we tread, as George Kennan wrote of the Soviet Union in 1950, on the "unfirm substance of the imponderables".[14] But the Russians seem more likely than not to avoid the worse possibilities that lie before them and achieve some at least of the better. Russia will make itself a healthier society than it is today and than the Soviet Union ever was. It may attain some at least of the predictability that goes with democracy, the rule of law and openness to the outside world. In time it will again play a significant role in the world's game.

Outsiders can only play a minor part in Russia's future. Britain is peripheral to Russia's major interests and can do little more than contribute to collective Western efforts. Boris Yeltsin's decision in 1997 to hold regular bilateral meetings with the French and German leaders but not with Britain is a salutary reminder of our limitations. Within the western camp, however, Britain has some advantages of its own. It has a major role to play in developing a firm but constructive western response to Russia's external ambitions. In NATO that role comes naturally and is familiar to British instincts. There is an equally important role for Britain in the development of the European Union's response to a nation which, partly European as it may be, is too big and too alien to find a place within the Union along with most of its European neighbours.

---

1   For a retrospective view of the cold war see John Lewis Gaddis, *We Now Know: Rethinking Cold War History* (Oxford: Oxford University Press, 1997).

2   Michael R Beschloss and Strobe Talbot, *At the Highest Levels. The Inside Story of the End of the Cold War* (Boston: Little Brown, 1993).

3   For the story as it developed over the centuries, see Geoffrey Hosking, *Russia: People and Empire* (London: Harper Collins, 1997); Orlando Figes, *A People's Tragedy* (London: Jonathan Cape, 1996); Isaac Deutscher, *Stalin, A Political*

Biography (Oxford: Oxford University Press, 1966); and David Remick, *Lenin's Tomb: The Last Days of the Soviet Empire* (New York: Random House, 1993).

4 John Lloyd, *Rebirth of a Nation* (London: Michael Joseph, 1998).

5 Richard Layard and John Parker, *The Coming Russian Boom* (New York: Free Press, 1996).

6 Daniel Yergin and Thane Gustafson, *Russia 2010* (London: Nicholas Brealey, 1994).

7 Stephen Handelman, *Comrade Criminal. The Theft of the Second Russian Revolution* (London: Michael Joseph, 1994).

8 Layard and Parker, *op. cit.*

9 Layard and Parker, *op. cit.*; Yergin and Gustafson, *op. cit.*

10 Zbigniew Brzezinski, *The Grand Chessboard* (New York: Basic Books, 1997).

11 Andrei S Markovits and Simon Reich, *The German Predicament. Memory and Power in the New Europe* (Ithaca: Cornell University Press, 1997).

12 Graham T Allison *et al., Avoiding Nuclear Anarchy, Containing the Threat of Loose Russian Nuclear Weapons and Fissile Material* (Cambridge, Mass.: MIT Press, 1997).

13 Heather Grabbe and Kirsty Hughes, *Eastward Enlargement of the European Union* (London: Royal Institute of International Affairs, 1997).

14 Cited in Yergin and Gustafson, *op. cit.*

11 Beyond the Tropic of Cancer

We have looked so far at Britain's dealings with familiar associates in North America and Europe, with the booming societies of east Asia, and with the old enemy Russia: two continents and much of a third. Chapter 9 examined British relationships with the world of Islam, extending right across Asia and into Africa, Europe and America. But a good third of the globe remains unvisited except through the Islamic connection. The countries of south Asia, Africa and Latin America and the island states of the Caribbean, the Indian Ocean and the Pacific are all of them places we used to lump together with more convenience than precision as the third world. Now we talk with a shade more discrimination of levels of development, yet for most of us they remain places of little interest. Nevertheless, each of them has a significance for Britain, as we have for them. Many of them first entered the world stage through British discovery and conquest: we have historic connections with them. Some promise to join east Asia's advance to prominence: we want to cooperate with them in exploiting the opportunities that that will bring. Many face desperate problems: we owe them our help in developing out of poverty. And all of them are part of inseparable humanity,[1] more alive to us today, when television brings us instantaneous pictures of each other's joys and woes, than when British adventurers, merchants, soldiers, missionaries and slave-traders first explored the world beyond the Tropic of Cancer.

As long as the stand-off between capitalism and Communism divided the northern hemisphere between the first world and the second, the third world accounted for most of the rest of the globe. It was shorthand that ignored great differences of policy, social and economic performance and prospects. But as they emerged from formal or informal colonialism 30, 40 and 50 years ago, the countries of Africa, of most of south Asia, Latin America and the island states were content to define themselves as "underdeveloped", "developing", or "in a state of development". The euphemisms meant that they looked to economic growth and to the social and political benefits that it would bring to give them modern nationhood and lift them out of the poverty, hunger and ill health that dogged their peoples' lives. The leaders of the third-world countries looked at the things they had in common, and sought to parlay them into a sense of international solidarity of the underprivileged and a global movement to attract attention to their concerns. They used the United Nations and its agencies, the Commonwealth and the Non-Aligned Movement as sounding boards for their needs and their view of world affairs. They formulated their ambitions in statements such as the five principles of Bandung, and the capitalist and Communist worlds, each eager to enlist them on its own side of the cold war or to keep them out of the camp of its opponents, made at least a show of positive response. The process wrote much of four decades of recent history.

The British had a large part in this. The empire ruled from London was dismantled and a Commonwealth in which third-world sovereign states predominated took its place.[2] Successive British governments tried to keep political and military power deployed around the world, to act as the United States' adjutant in holding Communism and nationalism in check, or to cover the imperial retreat. Modern British history is punctuated with third-world occasions: the withdrawal from Palestine, the partition of India, the Suez affair; Mau Mau in Kenya, the Emergency in Malaya and the confrontation with Indonesia; the presence East of Suez, the shambles in Aden, the winds of change in Africa, Rhodesia into Zimbabwe, natural disaster in the Caribbean.

Some Britons look back on that record with pride in an empire brought to a dignified finish. Many at the time saw it as an important component of Britain's decline and recalled Adam Smith's words on the loss of the first British empire, that in North America, after which Britain must "endeavour to accommodate her future views and designs to the real mediocrity of her circumstances".[3] For others the real truth about the process was that it was for too long a distraction from Britain's more vital interests nearer home. But on any view, these decades reiterated Britain's connections with most of the developing world, connections which for better or for worse matter still.

⤳

There was in fact always less solidarity about the non-aligned movement than its advocates pretend, and wide differences between the level of development, prospects and ambitions of its constituents. It stood nevertheless for a number of realities: emergence from colonialism, a new national pride, some sense of solidarity, reluctance to be enlisted in quarrels between East and West, and above all a persistent and overriding need to develop out of poverty. Other priorities often distracted attention from this last reality, but in the long run it was to prove inescapable. Some non-aligned countries mastered the art of economic and social development where others faltered. Today, as we have seen in Chapter 8, most of the countries of east Asia have graduated out of poverty, to become successful or promising industrialised states. Many of the oil-rich nations have achieved a status of their own, some of them as rich as Croesus. Parts of south Asia and Latin America are already following where east Asia has led, and others will tread the same path. The prospects for some island states could be reasonably good. But there remain, in Africa and in parts of south Asia and Latin America, many sovereign members of the United Nations with all the trappings of statehood which lack obvious natural comparative advantage and, apparently, the qualities which might lift them out of poverty. They present Britain and their other partners with widely differing prospects, both of problem and opportunity.

⤳

In a first group there are solid grounds for hope. This category embraces in particular south Asian, Latin American and a few African countries which are beginning to achieve comparative economic success, as east Asia has done in recent decades. India is pre-eminent among them, with a GDP at purchasing power parity already greater than that of Britain. Brazil's economy is almost twice the size of India's, with a population one-sixth of it. Mexico's, whether stimulated or imperilled by membership of the North American Free Trade Agreement, is not much smaller. Other countries hold comparable promise: big ones such as Pakistan and South Africa, small ones like Botswana and Mauritius.

There is no guarantee that these countries will follow east Asia into broad-based prosperity, any more than that east Asia's path will remain untroubled. Each has its great pools of the poor and underprivileged, and each faces major social tensions, exacerbated by the strains of economic change, by the demands of globalised markets and by the rising expectations that follow economic success. In each, the problems of corruption go hand in hand with change, distorting economic decision making and bringing politics into disrepute. India and its south Asian neighbours face in addition the difficulties of ethnic and religious dissension; and, externally, geopolitical difficulties that could destroy their hard-won economic successes. But all these countries – perhaps 20 of them in all in south Asia, Latin America and Africa – have it in them to grow towards prosperity over the next 20 years or so, join the industrialised world, build an extensive middle class and reduce the misery of their poverty-stricken majorities.

India, by every measure the greatest of them, has more than three times the population of the United States, an economy which is growing at more than 5 per cent per year, and real power in south Asia. Independent for half a century, it has able leaders, a dynamic business class, great intellectual resources and a skilled workforce prepared to work, for perhaps two generations more, for a comparative pittance. Industrialisation is giving India new resources and outlets. It could follow China and the rest of east Asia into industrial success. Some even believe that in the long run it will offer the rest of the developing world a better model than China, combining economic success with the democracy to which it has clung in face of difficulty ever since independence.

But India could succumb to the dangers that have threatened it ever since independence: the demands of an ever increasing, desperately poor population, religious and caste division, and corruption in politics, administration and business. Wherever India goes, its neighbours may go in its wake: Pakistan the ever-watchful rival, even poorer Bangladesh and Sri Lanka, whose prospects at independence seemed so much easier than the rest but which has in the event been riven by inter-communal destruction. Each will face problems as intense as India's, though often different: in Pakistan the clash between modernisation and fundamentalist Islam, in Bangladesh the pressures, even greater than elsewhere in south Asia, of over-population and climatic hazards; in Sri Lanka the continuing stand-off against the Tamil minority.

Change in south Asia is already beginning to put a quite different complexion on what has long been one of Britain's most important connections. If east Asia is Britain's true antipodes, south Asia is its intimate. Its problem is to ensure that links which go back more than two centuries, generating the largest and emotionally most complex of post-colonial love-hate relationships, are successfully adapted to modern circumstances.[4] That relationship still persists, expressed in major diasporas in Britain itself and in Britons – businessmen, aid workers, officials, advisers, bankers – working in the subcontinent. It is expressed also in large trade volumes; in continuing private investment and official aid; and in vigorous political dialogue. Direct investment, always substantial, is overtaking exports to the region as the chief expression of Britain's economic interest there. South Asia promises to be a leading growth area for British business. To increase our share in its economies is a major good to play for.

But the issues that face the countries of south Asia cannot be reduced to the problem of engendering the economic growth that could lead the region down east Asia's path. They also suffer from interlocking ethnic, religious, political and diplomatic problems that have distracted their attention from the question of development ever since independence.

India was established as an explicitly secular state. But from the very beginning the existence of Pakistan, just as explicitly Islamic, imposed strains on India's secularity. Bangladesh, when it broke away from Pakistan, retained its Islamic characteristics, if in a less assertive form. Now Islam's religious revival is taking increasingly political forms. Moslem self-awareness, what an outsider would call Islamic stridency, adds extra vigour to Pakistan's concern for Kashmir and for India's Moslem millions. It runs up squarely against a growing Hindu awareness and assertiveness, it too taking political and populist form, which threatens India's secularity and could undermine its democracy.

At the same time, the diplomatic context is shifting. For 40 years after independence, the Soviet Union was India's friend. China supported Pakistan; and through it obtained some *droit de regard* in south Asia. Now Russia's influence in south Asia is broken and what once seemed to be a threat to Pakistan from the north through Afghanistan has been lifted. China, on the other hand, is growing politically stronger and gathering diplomatic potency. In an exclusively subcontinental wrangle, Pakistan is no match for India, but a Pakistan backed diplomatically by China is another matter. No more than east Asia can south Asia assume that it can focus its concern solely on economic and social development, or that outsiders will leave it alone.

Britain's interests would be threatened by the instability that political or military tension in south Asia would bring. Even short of war there, nuclear proliferation in the area is dangerous in itself and as a signal to others. We would lose commercially from unrest within the south Asian countries, just as we stand to benefit from their development. And ethnic conflicts in the subcontinent could be viciously reflected on the streets of London and Birmingham. We have some capacity to influence events in the region. Our economic partnerships with the countries of the area give us some leverage. So do our historical experience and our generally good political reputation. The Commonwealth could play a helpful role if it were not blocked by the irreconcilability of the positions of India and Pakistan over Kashmir. However, of all the outside powers, only the United States and China have the capacity to play a leading hand in south Asia. If Britain feels that it should play more than a businessman's role there, it can only be as America's adjutant, or through the United Nations, the Commonwealth or the European Union.

～

The winding up of the old Indian Empire, for all the bloodshed that accompanied it, was a 20th-century success. The story of British policy in South Africa and Rhodesia was not. But we have regained influence there since the emergence of Zimbabwe and the fall of apartheid and now have a fairly strong position in southern Africa. Some of these countries, most notably South Africa itself, have the potential to achieve successful economic and social development. In a sense South Africa has already done so, with a strong mineral and industrial economy and a GDP per head ten times as high as India's. Its problem at home is to bind up the wounds of apartheid, satisfy the popular aspirations that its ending aroused, and ensure that its society, in many ways so hopeful, does not go the way of too many others in Africa. If it can do so it will become the first African country to achieve a rounded economic and political development and give all its people decent conditions of life.

At the same time, South Africa faces a second challenge, posed by expectations that it will take a leading role in Africa. In the south of the continent it is already doing so, but is finding its neighbours ambivalent about its efforts. Further afield, South Africa's material interests are not directly engaged, and commitment is more spasmodic. It has, for example, been reluctant to be drawn into a role in Zaire or into outright condemnation of the Nigerian regime. But if Britain is to undertake commitments in Africa that go beyond business and development assistance, South Africa's cooperation or at least understanding will be important.

~

In the 19th century and in the early years of this one, Britain was economically as involved in central and south America as in south Asia and southern Africa. But whereas in India the substance of the relationship was topped off with the facts of power and the pomp of empire, in south America an almost equally substantial relationship was conducted largely by sleight of hand. Nineteenth-century British naval power set free most of the Spanish American empire, but it is the Monroe Doctrine, purporting to close Latin America to the European powers, that is remembered. British money built the Argentinian railways and beef industry, but it was done without any shadow of political authority. The British imperial economy penetrated quite as deeply into South America as into Asia or Africa, but it was directed not from Whitehall but from the City.[5] The English language never began to replace Spanish and Portuguese, and only British Guiana, Belize and the Falkland Islands, each of them imperially insignificant, were coloured red upon the map. The liquidation of British overseas investment in the Second World War still further diminished its profile in the area.

Now, the countries of Latin America, like those of south Asia, stand at partings of ways. Brazil, Mexico and Chile promise to emulate east Asia and break fully into the global economy. They are going to become increasingly important powers, with Brazil, that continent of a country, staking a claim for permanent membership of the Security Council. A few other countries of the region may follow them, in increasing contrast to those which remain enslaved to economies which depend on a single crop, too often cocaine. In even the successful countries of Latin America there is a strong possibility that politics, dominated by the few, enlisted in the protection of privilege, will frustrate healthy development.

Latin America is not an area of first-class importance for Britain. The United States is the predominant outside influence, with individual European countries relatively insignificant beside it. Germany's industrial strength makes it a partial exception. So do the linguistic and cultural links of Spain and Portugal. Britain, its 19th-century role in the development of the continent now remote, has no obvious comparative advantage nor, the particular case of the Falkland Islands apart, interests other than economic ones there. We can take a share of growing markets, invest usefully, viewing the area as one not of concentration but of diversification. Like our European partners we can benefit from the desire throughout Latin America to keep inevitable dependency on the United States within bounds and to build links with the European Union to offset it.

⌒

The second category of country to be considered in this round-up of the world south of the Tropic of Cancer is that of the small island states. Most of them were brought into the world community by the chance of British discovery, colonisation and emancipation. They form over a third of the membership of the Commonwealth, getting on for a seventh of all the United Nations, yet they amount only to an infinitesimal proportion of humanity. Some of them, and particularly many of the Pacific islands, see their livelihoods threatened by Japanese driftnet fishing and their very existence by the sea-level rise that accompanies global warming. Others, especially in the Caribbean, have much that is needed for success in worldly terms: favourable climate and position, populations of a manageable size, a sound educational inheritance, the capacity to complement the bigger units of post-industrial society, and substantial diasporas. To the extent that they are failing to fulfil their potential, as too many of the West Indian islands are, they are a sad illustration of the damage that parochialism, corruption and violence can do to otherwise favoured places.

Failure would be a matter for these island states alone, if others did not exploit them. The most serious threat comes from organised crime, drug trafficking and money-laundering. The Caribbean has seen some absurd western interventions in the last 30 years: Britain's in Anguilla in the 1960s, America's in Grenada in 1983 and Panama in 1989. Each was motivated by the belief that these territories were falling victim to criminal minority movements that jeopardised western interests, whether stability on the United States' southern flank or the drugs that General Noriega was feeding to American students. The action in Panama still appears, nine years afterwards, absolutely indefensible; but it will be repeated if American interests are thought to be at risk. It is a useful and undemanding job for Britain in the Caribbean and in its other island ex-dependencies to provide the political and security back-up to keep criminal elements at bay and obviate the need for such interventions. It is a job worth doing for its own sake, and is given additional point by the continuing family links between the people of the islands and a large, articulate and assertive Afro-Caribbean community in Britain.

⌒

There remains a third category of nations in much of Africa and in parts of south Asia and Latin America whose situation can fairly be called desperate. These are countries which, poverty-stricken, lacking in natural resources, vulnerable to bad government or hostile climates or both, unable to take an effective part in a globalised world, fail year after year to deliver anything more than the basics of life to their inhabitants. Among them are the world's 20 poorest nations, 12 of them in Africa, on which Britain's overseas aid is concentrated; the countries threatened by population pressures or disease or desertification; the areas in which those whom Frantz Fanon called *"les damnés de la terre"* are disproportionately concentrated. In none of them are important British interests at stake, but in each of them, particularly its former colonies, Britain has obligations. How can we best reconcile obligation and interest?

We need, first, to see them as societies in their own right, recognising the diversity within and between them, avoiding an obsessive preoccupation with that single most prominent characteristic, poverty. There is much more to every one of them than their failure to be like us. What they are is the consequence of history, geography, ethnic background, religion and philosophy. To isolate their level of development or lack of it is as much an over-simplification as the preoccupation with bringing souls to Christ which drove some missionaries a century ago. If we are to be effective, in our own interest and theirs, we have to try to see each of these societies in the round.

We have to recognise also that we are bound to even the most remote of them. There is much more to this than the notion of the global village. The bond applies to bilateral relationships also. The links may derive from history, but today's circumstances nourish them too. We are experiencing the end of geography, the end of the sense of distance that used to shape attitudes to world affairs. Today we see African famine more quickly than we acknowledged starvation on the other side of the Irish Sea a century and a half ago. Indiscriminate logging in South America threatens the globe's environment and our own comfort. Marks & Spencer sell us flowers cut in Kenya 24 hours ago. Clerks in the Caribbean manipulate the electronic data of our insurance policies. The poorest of the developing countries are excluded from a say in world affairs yet deeply affected by them. No part of today's world has really fallen off the map.[6]

Both the industrialised world and the poorest countries waste too much time disputing who is to blame for the latters' afflictions. Colonialism bears some of the responsibility but it is a steadily declining one. So do the trading policies of the northern countries, where practice too often betrays free-trade principles. But with 30 or 40 years of independent statehood behind them, the leaders of the developing countries must bear much of the responsibility themselves. Their record, particularly in Africa, is a sorry one. Not all the developing world has been consumed by the ruling classes' autocracy, ineffectuality and corruption, but every part of it displays shocking examples of each of these characteristics. In the last ten years there have been attempts to do better, with free and reasonably fair elections in a few African countries, for example, with a search for accountability and transparency in government and business, and with a new concern for human rights. But Africa in particular seems to take a step back for every step it takes forward. Widespread Western disillusion with the developing world is an inevitable reaction.[7]

Yet the case for concerning ourselves with the poorest of the poor is unaffected by, perhaps even strengthened by, the failings of too many of their leaders. They have a legitimate call on our altruism, and charity in the best sense of the word has a part to play in our relationships with them. It is a thought that is much frowned upon: by the historian, who remembers Schwarzenberg glorying in his country's ingratitude;[8] by the diplomat in blinkered pursuit of his country's material interests; and today by ideologically driven market economists. It can be belittled, too, by psychologists, who see in altruism only the satisfaction of a more sophisticated form of self-interest, the desire for an easy conscience, for moral complacency. "Charity begins at home" remains a popular rule of thumb. But if altruism derives from perceptions of a common humanity,[9] it can draw no lines between humanity in this continent or that.

Yet many advocates of more generous policies towards the poorest countries believe that to justify overseas aid on altruistic grounds demotivates the donor and demeans the recipient. And there certainly are more utilitarian and, to some, more persuasive reasons than altruism for supporting the poorest countries of the developing world. Each of them is in a small way a market and usually a source of supply. Each has its vote at the United Nations, its geographical place, sometimes of strategic significance, on the globe. In despair, each is capable, as the countries of central Africa are demonstrating, of launching emigrants into a crowded world that does not want them but finds it hard to keep them out. The poor of the earth add their mite to environmental degradation. Their wild young men wreak terrorist mayhem, just as their farmers produce the drugs that destroy the minds of our sophisticated children. Third-world catastrophes prey on our peace of mind through television, capturing the latest war, famine and disease, the latest natural disaster. All these things serve to keep the developing world, if only fitfully, in our consciousness, reminding us of the damage that the weak and marginalised can do to our own more privileged lives. The amelioration of conditions there plays an integral part in the industrialised countries' defence of their own security.[10]

But these are not reasons for setting altruism aside. Nor are the arguments that aid is ineffective, black tyrants incorrigible, the poorest of the poor beyond hope. They are rather arguments for coupling altruism to intelligence, for more precisely directing our efforts to help. Donor countries and agencies are getting better at that, just as recipient countries are improving their standards. But volume is important too, and here we fail to meet our responsibilities. The disproportion between what Westerners spend on themselves and devote to helping others is an insult to man and a sin against God.[11] Year after year the countries of Europe and America, a few honourable exceptions apart, fall further short of the development assistance targets they have set themselves. Britain devotes 0.31 per cent of its GDP to official development assistance, against the United Nations target of 0.7 per cent. UNICEF tells us that what Europe spends annually on wine or the United States on beer would over a decade guarantee the basic essentials of life for the world's children.[12] The costs to the third world of the protection of northern agriculture and industry far outweigh the benefits of official development assistance: we deny the poor of the earth the opportunity to trade their way out of poverty.[13]

To some people, the structural adjustment programmes which the international financial institutions urge upon developing countries have real value; to others, they are part of the problem rather than the solution. Similarly, political, economic and environmental conditionalities present complex ethical and practical problems. So does the argument about forgiving debts that are not in any event going to be repaid. So does the power of the World Bank.[14] So sometimes do the activities of many international non-governmental organisations. The new

British government will encounter all these difficulties as it pursues its professed aim of giving ethical concerns a higher place in its foreign policy agenda. But it would be better placed in criticising the ethical standards of other governments if its own commitment to unashamed altruism in succouring the world's poor were clearer.

↬

Although much of the old third world grew out of the British empire, and although Britain had a major hand in the dealings which gave it its identity, there is no obvious single place in it for Britain today. The three categories of developing country described here differ widely from one another and in the opportunities and problems which they present. South Asia may go the way of east Asia, which may turn out to be the high road to developed prosperity or something considerably less. Latin America may achieve as much in a symbiotic relationship with north America. Both areas will essentially make their own stories, but in south Asia Britain has historical and economic advantages which can help it play a useful role. The island states offer an infinitely smaller stage, on which Britain may be able to play a useful part. The truly poor, especially in Africa, need all the help that the British can offer them. If they do provide help on a scale that matches the size of the problem, they can win advantages for themselves and head off developments that could damage them. But above all they will be doing something for nations which, for a variety of reasons, have difficulty in helping themselves, and doing it in large part out of an altruism of which they should not feel ashamed.

1   Shridath Ramphal, *Inseparable humanity, an anthology of reflections of Shridath Ramphal* (London: Hansib, 1988).

2   Denis Judd, *Empire. The British Imperial Experience from 1765 to the Present* (London: HarperCollins, 1996).

3   Cited in *Financial Times*, 27 June 1996.

4   A love-hate relationship of whose emotional intensity we were reminded by the Queen's visit to the subcontinent on the 50th anniversary of independence in 1997. See also V S Naipaul, *India. A Million Mutinies Now* (London: Heinemann, 1990).

5   P J Cain and A G Hopkins, *British Imperialism. Innovation and Expansion 1688–1914* (London: Longman, 1993).
6   For three valuable if widely ignored analyses of this interdependence see the Brandt Report, *Global Challenge* (London: Pan, 1985); the Brundtland Report, *Our Common Future* (Oxford: Oxford University Press, 1987); and the Carlsson/Ramphal Report, *Our Global Neighbourhood* (Oxford: Oxford University Press, 1995). The Commonwealth has also done useful work on the subject, notably the Brown Report, *Change for the Better* (London: Commonwealth Secretariat, 1991).
7   Keith B Richburg, *Out of America. A black man confronts Africa* (New York: Basic Books, 1997).
8   "Austria will astound the world with the magnitude of her ingratitude", Felix, Prince Schwarzenberg, on Russian help to Austria, 1849.
9   Kristen Renwick Monroe, *The Heart of Altruism* (Princeton: Princeton University Press, 1996).
10 James Morton, *The Poverty of Nations: the Aid Dilemma at the Heart of Africa* (London: I B Tauris, 1996).
11 See Peter Unger's aptly titled book, *Living High and Letting Die* (Oxford: Oxford University Press, 1997).
12 P and L Adamson, *The State of the World's Children* (Oxford: Oxford University Press, 1993).
13 Pat Simmons, *Words into Action: Basic Rights and the Campaign against World Poverty* (London: Oxfam, 1996).
14 Catherine Caufield, *Masters of Illusion. The World Bank and the Poverty of Nations* (London: Macmillan, 1997).

12   The new danger list

The issues discussed earlier in this book lend themselves to explicit packaging. But the world is faced with many others which do not. They are issues which matter, but on which we have not yet imposed any tidy intellectual order. They make headlines, fade away and then again seize public attention. From time to time terrorism impinges violently on our consciousness; then, as memory of the individual horror fades, we are left only with the old routines to protect us against a repetition. Our emotions are aroused by natural disaster, or by man-made disaster such as war, famine and the flight of refugees. We see our commercial interests put in the balance against a concern to punish human rights. The newspapers tell us that Russian nuclear scientists or international arms dealers are beyond the control of national and international authority, proliferating dangerous know-how and equipment around the world. Narcotics dealers, money launderers, the corrupters of international business pose different threats which in their own way are as dangerous. And the impersonal threat of environmental degradation looms over all our futures.

Some of these problems are new ones, the product of technological and social change or the unwelcome consequences of the end of the cold war. Others have roots in imperial days, in the industrial revolution, or in the first assertions of democracy. Many only seem new, because they come to us repackaged. Many have connections with issues discussed already in this book. But it is worth bringing them together for separate discussion, because they confront Britain, like other national societies, with the need to take positions on unfamiliar issues.

Together they constitute a security agenda different from that of mutually assured destruction, tank armies and nuclear submarines.

~

The first issue is the domestic behaviour of foreign states. To address it at all calls in question a basic traditional doctrine of international relations. It holds that states do not interfere in other states' domestic affairs, any more than a gentleman enquires about the state of his neighbour's bank account. It is enshrined in Article 2 (7) of the United Nations charter. That article has been much reinterpreted, and gradually its full rigour has been eroded, but strictly interpreted it would keep the United States out of Northern Ireland as much as the Commonwealth out of Nigeria. Its principles die hard. Throughout the cold war, when the great powers meddled in the internal affairs of their neighbours they did so under the cloak either of hypocrisy or of plausible deniability.

Yet the doctrine of non-intervention is not practised with consistency. Apartheid in South Africa aroused a global concern to force change. The West cried out against Soviet treatment of Sakharov and against the 1989 massacre in Tiananmen Square. Moscow and Beijing were as raucous in condemning the West's post-colonial imperialism. Human rights monitoring has been routine for 20 years now, and in the Conference on Security and Co-operation in Europe East and West accepted in practice outside interest in their internal affairs. For the Scandinavian countries it has been second nature to combine generosity as aid-givers with righteous criticism of developing countries' human rights records. Amnesty International has made itself an international authority on domestic evils. Press, television and e-mail spread internationally the word of atrocity within national boundaries, and public opinion demands action in response.

There are good arguments for interference. One is that the freedoms necessary to build civil societies are the key to economic development also. It is argued that aid should be traded off against environmental good behaviour, debt forgiveness against the rooting out of corruption. Governments, constrained by practicalities – and by the knowledge that they live in glass houses themselves – show more restraint than press or public opinion. International business feels jeopardised by the impracticable righteousness of its critics. But the desire to pry into the domestic doings of other nations has long overtaken the traditional conventions of international intercourse.

At least three things are imperilled by the erosion of the principles which underlie Article 2 (7). The first is the hard-won civility of peace-time dealings between sovereign states, in most circumstances prefer-able to megaphone diplomacy. The second is the principle, however ridiculous dictatorships can make it seem, that it is for national societies to choose their own form of government and not for others to instruct them. The third is the benefit that international trade can bring to buyer and seller, to good bilateral relations and to world development, now so often put at risk by the political view that government, press or public takes of a trading partner's domestic behaviour.

The British, like everyone else, have difficulty in deciding where they will strike the balance between all these considerations. The Labour government emphasises its heightened concern for ethical con-siderations but is finding difficulty in expressing it consistently.[1] The contradictions are more acute for us than they are for some of our part-ners. We are heavily dependent on international trade, and exception-ally deeply involved in an arms trade that is the first thing to be called in question when we discuss the ethical content of foreign policy. We have a practical faith in the benefits of international contact, diplo-matic, commercial or personal. If we have exported our own system of government to half the Commonwealth, it has been done by consent rather than coercion. We have an instinct and an interest in keeping our noses out of others' domestic business. But at the same time the British people have active social consciences and a developed interest in the outside world. Their inherited instinct to act as nanny to the world is by no means entirely ridiculous. They are served by a media quick to uncover foreign undoing and to denounce the government's hypocrisy when it condones it. In instance after instance, these factors outweigh the other side of the argument. We condemn and we act upon our condemnation.

In practice British decisions are more likely to be guided by the cir-cumstances of the individual instance than by general principles. But Britain would be well advised to incline to the traditional, conservative, non-interventionist approach. The short-term commercial arguments for doing so are obvious. For instance, why risk a share of the Chinese market to protest against the imprisonment of a dissident? There is also the longer-term argument for maintaining contact. In the cold war it rightly kept us in close working contact with the Soviet Union, whose record on human rights and accountability fell short of any western standard. We cannot afford to be more sensitive about China's sins. There is, too, the argument for consistency, because there is no defensible consistency once you have started down the path of regulating international contact by reference to domestic behaviour: can you condemn capital punishment in Saudi Arabia but not in the United States? It is a fact, finally, that by somebody's standards none of us is in a position to cast the first stone.

There will of course be exceptions. Televised atrocity can inflame world opinion to the point where the cry that something must be done rightly outweighs the conventional wisdom of discretion. Where countries have committed themselves to agreed benchmarks, as in the Commonwealth, their partners should hold them to them.[2] And to attach to official development assistance conditionalities which are directly relevant to its effective use raises different issues from the manipulation of trade policy and from trade sanctions. But the rule of thumb remains: in a tense and interdependent world, political, commercial and human contact is too precious to subordinate to the search for the mote in your neighbour's eye. There is no contradiction between such pragmatism and the more generous, altruistic approach to the developing world advocated in the previous chapter, although the two arguments may appeal to the emotions of very different constituencies.

The United Nations offers ways of blunting the dilemma which this issue undoubtedly presents.[3] It can give legitimacy to action against domestic behaviour which is unacceptable to the world community, as it did in the aftermath of Desert Storm, although much less easily than to action against clear international transgression, like the original invasion of Kuwait. There are ways of making the process easier, such as that suggested by the Commission on Global Governance,[4] which would give a right of petition to the United Nations itself to individuals and non-state actors. There is general recognition that the world has ceased to be the simple, state-based place it seemed to the United Nations' founding fathers. It is the very permeability of frontiers, unimaginable in 1945, which today provokes one nation to seek to pass judgment on another and which creates the dilemma we have discussed. That same permeability, expressed in changes within the United Nations, may help to resolve it.

⤚

States present the world community with another form of difficulty: the problems that arise when a state collapses, polity and society fall apart, and the chaos and misery which ensue lead to calls for international intervention. For example, the former Yugoslavia's dissolution opened up the problems of Serbian-Croatian war, Serbian aggression and civil war in Bosnia, and the continuing possibility of collapse in Macedonia and Kosovo. In central Africa, Rwanda, Burundi and Zaire have experienced comparable miseries, as in west Africa have Liberia and Sierra Leone. In each case crossborder and ethnic differences play a part, but in all these tragedies there is little of the clarity of international law and of interest which made the world's rescue of Kuwait so clearcut an operation.[5]

Britain has a big part in addressing these problems. It brings to them particular assets: a permanent Security Council seat, vigorous diplomacy, its international relief and development agencies, and armed forces practised in the kind of intervention that the consequences of state failure demand. But each of these assets is also a potential danger, provoking us to take a position and tempting us to action in circumstances where, as in central or west Africa, there is little specifically British interest to be discerned. Britain will not be able to escape involvement in the next collapse that requires emergency international attention, but it has a major interest in reducing the costs and increasing the chances of success by putting in place a properly structured system of anticipating and coping with the problems of the failed state.

The first principle should be a commitment to the preventive diplomacy that can help prevent such problems arising in the first place. States with strong political institutions, good economic prospects and a developed civil society are unlikely to collapse. International action, both official and voluntary, can help them achieve these goods. Its cost to the developed world is a fraction of the cost of the emergency intervention, peace-keeping and peace enforcement which are necessary when a state breaks up. The self-interest of avoiding being drawn into the costly, dangerous and often insoluble problems of a failed state stands beside altruism and commercial self-interest as an argument for more development assistance to the countries of the old third world.

The second principle is prompt action when things go wrong. Many difficulties stand in the way: the cost of keeping an intervention capacity, civilian and military, in being; the difficulty of establishing the facts of a deteriorating situation; the delays inherent in securing agreement to intervention by the government and the parties concerned. The last Secretary-General of the United Nations called for the establishment under United Nations control of a small standing intervention force.[6] The idea goes right back to the organisation's founding fathers, but its relevance is even greater today than it was when East-West rivalry inhibited effective action. It could provide the muscle to support action, authorised by the United Nations, by regional organisations such as the Organisation of African Unity. But sceptics point to the failure of the United Nations in Bosnia and argue that only the major powers and NATO have the organisational capacity and strength to act effectively in failed states. Nevertheless, the proposal deserves British backing, both in argument and, if the force is not restricted to non-Security Council powers, in kind.

In an organisation deep in debt, with many of its members, including the most powerful of them all, the United States, in default on their subscriptions, the standing force will not come into being tomorrow, if at all. Britain will continue to be faced with demands to take national action to rescue failed states. Its next principle must be selectivity, responding positively only where there is a prospect of effective action by a substantial cross-section of nations acting under United Nations authority. United States involvement will often be indispensable, but France is the world's most active peace-keeper. The other major European powers have the capacity but more inhibitions. Smaller European countries, particularly in Scandinavia, have civil and military capacity to offer. Europe can often take the lead. Many Commonwealth countries have a long peace-keeping record and attitudes, training and doctrine in common with Britain. There is a justified hesitation about involving the Commonwealth as an organisation in peace-keeping and enforcement, but cooperation by a number of countries within it presents fewer difficulties.

It is, however, important to avoid an over-militarised approach. Military capacity on the ground may be necessary, and when the situation has deteriorated beyond a certain point it must be war-fighting capacity, as experience in Bosnia illustrates. But the farce of the United States' operations in Somalia demonstrates the dangers of getting drawn into warfare that serves no useful purpose. So British intervention requires not merely effective international cooperation, but cooperation too between the civil and military arms of government, and with the non-governmental organisations that deliver so much of the humanitarian assistance that these situations require.

Britain must also recognise the need to balance humanitarian considerations against the more political. Recent interventions have repeatedly run up against their frequent incompatibility. The public demands action to feed the starving and house the homeless, but humanitarian action can easily hinder political effectiveness, by providing safe havens to wrong-doers, as in central Africa or Cambodia, or by turning peace-keepers or aid workers into hostages, as in Bosnia. Effective intervention requires a clear political concept, not easily arrived at in situations of chaos and confusion. It needs to have a long-term perspective, extending beyond the immediate relief of an intolerable situation.

⌐

Britain like the rest of the world faces other problems that scarcely troubled its policy-makers half a century ago. The environment as an international concern is pre-eminent among them. It is scarcely imaginable now that environmental issues were first discussed in a full-scale international conference only 26 years ago, at the United Nations Stockholm environment conference of 1972. It has grown to attract the attention of expert commissions, governments, world organisations and global conferences; it is a major topic of international business.[7]

Environmental threats are universal but they bite differently in different places. Britain's position is relatively favourable. Climate change will probably affect it less drastically than countries in many other parts of the world. It still has energy resources of its own greater than most of its European neighbours. Its food supplies are well diversified. Its development has moved beyond dependency on environmentally damaging heavy industry. But these are minor advantages by comparison with the common exposure Britain shares with the rest of mankind. Moreover, it is vulnerable to the charge that it takes more than its share of the globe's resources. It is fanciful to imagine that we could contract out of international action to save the environment.[8]

At the moment Britain is well regarded among those who acknowledge the reality and importance of the threat. It claims quite a good record in improving its national environmental performance, although this improvement is heavily dependent on the shift from the use of coal in power generation to the finite resource of North Sea natural gas. But it is not immune from pressures which all the industrialised countries face in tackling the environmental challenge, such as concern for economic growth and jobs and attachment to consumer toys such as the package holiday and the motor car. Like the others it takes two steps forward and one step back in its environmental performance. It recognises the need for international action and takes its domestic achievements and shortcomings to be praised and criticised at conference after international conference. The need for international action emerges ever more signally. In discussion of it at least two areas of strategic difference repeatedly emerge.[9]

The first is the extreme exposure of parts of the underdeveloped world to the threats of environmental degradation. Some island states face extinction by sea-level rise. The countries of the Sahel are threatened by creeping desertification. Other developing countries have environmental assets, notably what is left of the tropical rain forests, valuable both as resources to be sustained and as international bargaining chips. But on balance the environmental threat which most of the peoples of the third world face is worse than that which confronts the industrialised countries.[10] As the Rio Earth Summit in 1992 acknowledged, massive resource transfers from the industrial world are needed if they are to have any chance of meeting it; yet five years later, at the follow-up meeting in Kyoto, the world was forced to recognise that they were not being made.

The second is the accelerating impact on the global environment of growth and industrialisation in countries in economic transition such as China and India. The developed world and above all the United States impose a disproportionate load on the environment. But industrialisation on the back of fossil fuels is already transforming east Asia, and particularly China, into a major polluter; and industrialisation in south Asia and Latin America will add to the globe's burden. To a degree, modern technology can help these countries bypass the Satanic Mills era of industrialisation, but rising standards of living for millions will take an inescapable toll. Clean nuclear power presents a new range of problems of its own, often more emotional than rational. The inevitable result of the spread of industry-based prosperity must be a clash of environmental interests between the satisfied nations such as Japan, the United States and western Europe and the demanding new industrial nations of the world.

Britain has no particular position of its own on all this, beyond an instinct and an interest to seek responsible solutions and a strong scientific base in contributing to finding them. But it needs to argue for an imaginative and generous commitment by the industrialised powers to help the rest of the world to face up to its environmental challenges. For in this field above all others, effective solutions will be international ones. They will, once again, trench on the individual state's ability to go its own sovereign way untrammelled by the interests and concerns of others.

⌒

Environmental problems exacerbate other issues which already threaten large portions of the globe, amongst which population growth is prominent. In Africa this has pretty well negated the benefits that economic growth might have brought since independence. In much of south Asia and Latin America it stands in the way of growth out of extreme poverty. It is provoking more and more communities to seek escape in migrations which heighten ethnic tensions and provoke more fortunate societies, particularly in Europe, to pull up the drawbridge against new immigrants. Overpopulation intensifies mankind's demands on finite natural resources: food, water, energy and living space.[11]

With a stable population and no significant doctrinal objections to family limitation, Britain contributes little to the problem and something – through development assistance, investment and trade – to ameliorating it. The same is true of other issues which escape national definition or packaging, such as problems of health and disease, of ethnicity and gender. None directly impinges on Britain's interests in any major way; each affects the world to which Britain's interests are linked. AIDS is a serious if exaggerated national concern, and some at least of its origins are international. Plague and new variants on old diseases could pose an infinitely greater threat. Ethnic differences continue to afflict many parts of the world, and have some lodgement in multi-ethnic Britain. Discrimination against women is in many developing countries a major obstacle to growth out of poverty. As for migration, which faces the world with increasingly serious challenges – and often tragedies – Britain has made itself largely secure against the assaults of immigrants and refugees, but at a severe price to national self-respect.

All these problems pose for Britain a fundamental question about its involvement in the outside world. In other matters it has no choice: its interests cry out for international security arrangements, for international trade and for the coordination of a multiplicity of issues through the European Union, the World Trade Organisation and the IMF. But world population, hunger, ethnic tension, migration – these are issues which might seem to pass it by. Has Britain, beyond an altruistic commitment to helping the less fortunate, any serious part to play in tackling such problems?

If it has, the case for doing so flows in part from historical and human obligation and in part from interest. Our history has involved us in more of the world than any other single nation. We are aware of other countries to an unusual degree. Interests and obligations intertwine. In Mumbai we want to do business with the merchant princes; we cannot quite ignore its poor. In Latin America we want to sell to the middle classes; we cannot pass its street-children by. We have too the same, more general interest in helping the third world that we have examined in Africa, and in states at risk of failure. It is in our interest to avoid the suffering that can lead to disorder and chaos, and so destabilise great areas of the globe. This argument is not just altruism dressed up as hard-headed self-interest, but a reflection of costs and benefits. When the leaders of developing countries say that order in their countries is a first-world interest, they are both threatening us with chaos if we do not help them and pointing to the indivisibility of humanity. Many of the countries threatened by exclusion from the magic circles of growth and prosperity are particularly linked with Britain, through history and through political, economic and human connections. We should help them overcome the problems of hunger, disease and conflict that threaten too many of them.

＊

Seven years after the collapse of the Soviet Union, Britain has few formal enemies. A few maverick states – Libya, Iraq, Iran, North Korea – may be dangerous. For historical reasons others have reason to dislike us – more often perhaps than we like to admit. But most of the serious international dangers that threaten our well-being come not from states but from groups and individuals operating outside the law. As much as business or good works, crime has become globalised. One criminal network starts with narcotics and leads through money-laundering to the accumulation of vast economic power with the capacity to threaten the stability of smaller nations.[12] Another traffics in arms, particularly from the former Soviet Union. In many of the countries in transition and in the developing world, crime and corruption – the latter too often originating in the industrialised countries – threaten legitimate business and distort politics and administration. Non-state violence – terrorism to the victims, sometimes heroic idealism in the eyes of its perpetrators – haunts the world's airports, ministerial offices and city streets.

Britain shares the general interest in combating these crimes. The IRA has taught us the hard way many lessons in combating non-state violence. The City's position at the centre of the world's spider's web of money gives us a special interest in dealing with money-laundering. The island states and colonies of the Caribbean are vulnerable to drug trafficking and the money power that goes with it: Britain has a direct interest in helping local governments to combat them. Some British companies, particularly in the arms industry, in high technology and in contracting, operate in fields where corruption of ministers and officials to win a contract is commonplace. Britain's interest in checking international crime is obvious. Nuclear or chemical weapons in irresponsible hands could threaten us directly. Countries that collapse under the weight of criminality lose us hopes of export markets and lucrative investment. Narcotics are a menace on our domestic streets. Non-state violence, whatever the cause it serves, is a direct threat to British lives and property.

So here again are causes that draws us into international cooperation, and thus into mutual dependencies which limit further our sovereign choices. But in each case the logic of the situation which drives us down that road cannot be evaded. In yesterday's world we learned the hard way the necessity to unite against the old security dangers. Unity, cooperation, mutual dependency are equally necessary if we are to fight the new ones.

1 Statement by the Foreign and Commonwealth Secretary, 12 May 1997
2 For example, in the Harare Commonwealth Declaration of October 1991.
3 Some are documented in Nigel Rodley (ed.), *To Loose the Bands of Wickedness, International Intervention in Defence of Human Rights* (London: Brassey's, 1992).
4 *Our Global Neighbourhood* (Oxford: Oxford University Press, 1995).
5 For some modern historical background see Anthony Parsons, *From Cold War to Hot Peace, UN Interventions 1947–1994* (London: Michael Joseph, 1995) and for an assessment of the present position Michael Dugh (ed.), *The UN, Peace and Force* (London: Cass, 1997).
6 Boutros Boutros Ghali, *Agenda for Peace* (New York: United Nations, 1992).
7 Tony Brenton, *The Greening of Machiavelli* (London: Royal Institute of International Affairs, 1994).
8 Duncan McLaren, Simon Bullock and Nusrat Yousuf, *Tomorrow's World: Britain's Share in a Sustainable Future* (London: Earthscan, 1997).
9 Lorraine Elliott, *The Global Politics of the Environment* (London: Macmillan, 1998).
10 Martin Holdgate *et al.*, *Climate Change. Meeting the Challenge* (London: Commonwealth Secretariat, 1989).
11 Lester R Brown *et al.*, *State of the World 1998* (London: Earthscan, 1998).
12 For a graphic account see Jeffrey Robinson, *The Laundrymen: Inside Money Laundering, the World's Third Largest Business* (New York: Arcade, 1996).

13   Rules and referees

The first chapter of this book explored some of the international factors that challenge the pre-eminence of the state. International and regional organisations, international business and philanthropy, people-to-people contact around the globe, all compete with it for influence. So does the technological change that has eaten away the significance of physical distance and largely rendered national boundaries irrelevant. Yet these forces have far to go to create an international order on which nations, peoples and individuals can rely. We have to ask ourselves what can be done to promote some kind of world order that will do more good than harm in our global village.

You can look at the history of the search for order from many standpoints. Empires from the Babylonian to the British have imposed rough-and-ready discipline on large parts of the known world. In our century the internationalist has put his faith in world institutions: the League of Nations after the First World War and the United Nations after the Second. Traditionalists look back to harsher and more muscular disciplines: the concert of nations which kept Europe more or less in order throughout the 19th century and the cold war stand-off which preserved the peace for most of the second half of the 20th.

With the collapse of Communism came a spasm of optimism about the value of both approaches. The United Nations was belatedly entering into its inheritance: at last it could play the role its founding fathers had envisaged. The United States, victor in the cold war and benevolent imperialist, would give a world that had reached the end of history a New World Order.[1] Both approaches came together for a brief moment of triumph in the Gulf war, with the United States and its allies repelling aggression and restoring order in the name of the United Nations. Disillusion soon followed.

∽

Britons with a historical turn of mind see their country's role as central in providing the world with order over the last three centuries. You do not need rose-tinted spectacles to discern a record of value to the world. With all their faults, British exploration, settlement and conquest brought order of a kind to the globe. Britain coordinated the world's resistance to Napoleon, and so made possible the Concert of Europe. In the 19th century it turned an adventurers' empire into something more formal and beneficent, bringing order to a large part of mankind. In the 20th century it fought two assaults on world order and helped keep Communism at bay. It vacated its empire in a reasonably orderly fashion and put the Commonwealth in its place. It was vigorous in support of the efforts of both the United Nations and the United States to police the world. So it is not self-delusion for the British to ask whether this record does not give them a special historical place in the search for global order even today. How the question is answered is key to the solution of the broader question of where in the world their country belongs.

But it is not self-evident that Britain in the future should engage itself in the search for global order, in the leading role which its historical record suggests. The isolationist can argue that we should pull up the drawbridge over our island moat. The argument is more cogent in this field, where some at least of the case to the contrary depends on altruistic considerations, than where quantifiable British interests such as trade would suffer if we confined ourselves to the cultivation of our garden. The more moderate sceptic argues that Britain must do its bit for world order, but in a minor role, pleading inadequate resources and historical inhibition, claiming only a modest place suitable to our diminished economic status, sheltering not just behind the United States but behind economically more powerful countries such as Germany and Japan as well. There is suspicion of international action for action's sake, of "punching above our weight" for no good contemporary reason. And there is a powerful, if tendentious, argument for tackling our own domestic shortcomings before we go out to correct other peoples'.

There are strong arguments that point the other way, but they are best explored not head-on, but by way of an examination of the instruments available to keep the world's peace. They are four in number. The first is the coalition of industrialised nations which gathers around the United States. The second and third are the United Nations and the Commonwealth. The fourth is more tenuous, less instantly recognisable, but perhaps just as real: that amalgam of commercial interest, non-governmental action, private charity and a myriad of individual responses which has already started to produce an integrated world community.

∽

The first of these instruments, the grouping round the United States which might be called the OECD coalition, appeals to powerful British instincts. Its long-term track record is good, all the way from destroying Hitler and Japan, through containing Communism, to the Gulf war and to decisive, if belated, action in Bosnia. It has resources; the wealth and the diplomatic and military muscle of the industrialised world. Its effectiveness is not hampered by the different approaches of peoples with quite different backgrounds and conflicting interests. It gives Britain if not a starring then at least a leading supporting role, which our diplomats and soldiers have shown they can fill with confidence and distinction.

In practical terms, this OECD coalition is going to have an indispensable role to play in keeping the world on the rails. Regional organisations and ad hoc regional coalitions can cope with lesser security problems, but big challenges require real force to deal with them. There may be more Gulf crises, more Bosnias; and for 20 years at least only the United States and NATO will have the military muscle that will be required to resolve them. The coalition is the Atlantic world's surest instrument in protecting its own interests, and the most effective way of expressing Western policies.

But if this coalition is going to remain necessary to world order, it will not be sufficient to do the job on its own. It suffers from infirmity of purpose. The United States itself is uncertain, its interest episodic and its attention span limited; and if, sometime early in the next century, the lead were to pass to the European Union or Japan, they would prove themselves infirm of purpose too. The coalition's effectiveness is hampered also by the suspicions of others: Russia, conscious of humiliation at NATO's hands, the Moslem world fearing new Crusades, Africans suspicious of new colonialism and Asians who question western values. Above all, it lacks the legitimacy that global organisations can claim, because it represents at best only the West's good intentions for other people and at worst only western interests.

There are good grounds for some of these suspicions. The United States may be the world's most powerful policeman, but its objectivity is often questionable. It sees too many world problems in terms that do no more than project on to them its own domestic prejudices. Too often, it plays favourites, as with Israel and Egypt, or demonises enemies, such as Cuba, Libya and Iran. The United States has vast practical authority, but its actions frequently call its moral authority in question. Yet no other member of the OECD coalition is without sin, and even if one were it would lack the power necessary to take the United States' place.

So the coalition of industrial powers is an imperfect instrument. But there can be little question of the need for it to project power and accept responsibilities, or of Britain's prominent place in it if it chooses to take it. Britain has the necessary knowledge of the world, historically based but drawing on a broad range of contemporary contacts. It has the political and diplomatic skills, expressed as much in the Security Council and General Assembly as in some tragic corner of Africa or the former Yugoslavia. It has consistently available and usable armed forces which today only France can match. And the British people seem to be willing to back overseas commitments where global order is threatened.

But the British quite reasonably want to weigh the costs of such commitments and to share the risks with partners. In Bosnia they have seen the fallibility of the European Union, but they acknowledge the need to build up a capacity for Europe to act in some circumstances without the United States. Hence the search to give the Western

European Union greater effectiveness and to improve bilateral co-ordination, particularly with France. But major challenges still require the involvement of the United States, most effectively through NATO and its British-led Rapid Reaction Force. These policies, difficult as they are to put across to the public, can secure domestic support for involvement in a collective effort where British interests are at risk, where there is a will on the ground to find a settlement, and where televised tragedy demands action by those who have the capacity to take it.

∽

The United Nations displays a very different assembly of strengths and weaknesses. Where the OECD coalition has well-organised instruments such as NATO at its disposal, the United Nations is frequently chaotic. Where the coalition can deploy coordinated diplomacy, it must get by with makeshift systems. It is anybody's guess whether the Secretary-General's efforts at reform will improve things, or whether its members will give it the consistent support it needs. Nevertheless, where the OECD coalition can speak only for one part of world society, the United Nations has the legitimacy that comes from universality. However inadequately, it represents all the nations and all the peoples. In a perfect world, it is through the United Nations that the peoples of the earth would express their collective will.

Yet from its very beginnings the United Nations has been hampered, often hamstrung, by the imperfections of its members.[2] The wartime allies who founded the organisation saw it as a way to avoid war and as a vehicle for their own international authority. To the emerging nations it was a means of shifting the balance of world power in their favour, and the split between East and West gave them extra diplomatic leverage. Corruption became inherent in the organisation and was reinforced by tensions between its members. It broke repeated efforts to bring about reform and give the United Nations relevance to changing circumstances.

Nevertheless, throughout the cold war, no one – not even the United States or the Soviet Union – dared to give the United Nations its quietus.[3] And with the end of the cold war it looked as if its time of fulfilment had come. With the end of great power rivalry there would be an end to vetoes of each other's proposals for United Nations action. Enriched by their peace dividends, its members could at last endow it with the resources it needed. A world at last set free to change and to express itself would give the organisation ample opportunities to prove its mettle.

Almost at once, as if on cue, Saddam Hussein's seizure of Kuwait provided an occasion to test these propositions. The United States extended the Western coalition to bring most of the Moslem world into the alliance against Saddam. It secured United Nations cover for its actions. The Iraqi invaders were sent miserably packing. The operation and its aftermath revealed numerous shortcomings, but it demonstrated that in certain specific circumstances at least the global community could organise itself to protect a new world order. And it did so in effect by bringing together the resources and leadership of the United States' OECD club with the consent and support of the world as expressed in the Security Council.

Disillusion quickly followed. The new world order demonstrated a surer touch in repelling attacks across national borders than in protecting Saddam Hussein's own people. It showed itself markedly less decisive in crises where there was no threat to the developed world's oil supplies. Somalia revealed the shortcomings of the American approach to peace-keeping and the inability of others to take the United States' place. The tragedies of Croatia and Bosnia demonstrated the inability of the United Nations, of the Western European Union, of the European Union and of the Organisation for Security and Co-operation in Europe to tackle outbreaks of aggression, civil war and atrocity at Western Europe's back door. This was a multifaceted failure which only belated United States intervention and NATO muscle could reverse.

The years which followed triumph in the Gulf consumed faith in the United Nations and hope for a new world order. The world lurched from one threat to order, security or human rights to another. In each instance instruments of the United Nations proved themselves inadequate to the tasks they were set. Good and able men and women in its service struggled in impossible circumstances with inadequate means. In frightening displays of political indiscipline, the member

states, and particularly the United States, compounded the organisation's difficulties. They heaped on it the blame for their own shortcomings and denied it the resources it needed. Their criticism whipped
up nationalistic resentment of the United Nations, while their outspoken contempt corroded its self-confidence. Between them they
created an entirely false antithesis between the OECD coalition and the
United Nations. Yet one crisis after another demonstrated that the
world still needed the services of the United Nations, its agencies such
as UNICEF and the High Commission for Refugees, and its economic
parallels such as the World Bank and the IMF. Imperfect as they were,
they alone could claim global legitimacy, and the world had no substi-
tute to put in their place.

⌐

Britain has picked its way through the wreckage of the world's attempts to create a new international order as skilfully as most, and with
more distinction than some of its partners. It has made its choices pragmatically, with scarcely an overarching rationale in sight, and if at times
its posture has been a sorry one, the reason has usually been the sheer
intractability of the situation. For all the criticism of its failures, Britain
is better placed than most to contribute to the search for a global order
that makes coherent sense.

It is, in the first place, a committed member both of the OECD
coalition and of the United Nations, and it has managed to keep the
demands of both in balance. In the absence of the United States it took
the lead with France in trying to build an effective United Nations operation in Bosnia, and learned the hard way the limitations of lightly
armed peace-keepers. When the United States took action, Britain was
close behind it in making NATO intervention effective. So it has
learned that although there may be situations in which the United
Nations can act alone, and that there are others where only American-
led muscle will suffice, most of the world's problems of security and
order demand multiple involvements: peace-keepers, election monitors, aid agencies, human rights protectors, peace enforcers and all too
often war crimes prosecutors.

Second, as a permanent member of the Security Council, Britain has a vested interest in making the United Nations' control and supervisory machinery work. It recognises the need to build consensus within the Council and maximum support in the General Assembly. And it benefits from a fact that we have noticed before: its unrivalled range of international connections. The Commonwealth plays a part in this, as do the English language, the broad spread of Britain's diplomatic representation, its international business interests and the extent of Britain's intellectual interests in distant places.[4]

Can Britain do more to make the United Nations a more effective instrument of global order? It pays its dues in full and on time. It plays an active part in the work of the organisation and gives the Secretary-General and his colleagues the comfort (and at times the embarrassment) of vigorous diplomatic interaction. It has been in the forefront of efforts to improve the organisation's efficiency. But realism suggests that in any body representative of all mankind, with 185 member governments intent on diverting its efforts into channels that best serve their interests, a body moreover staffed by individuals of a cacophony of nationalities – some internationalist idealists, more servants of the countries from which they come, too many of them intent in the first instance on their personal advantage – effectiveness will always be a relative concept and only spasmodically achieved.

The United Nations was brought into existence as an instrument to ameliorate relationships between states. It was to be the servant of its members. The state remained sovereign, and retained all essential initiative. Now, 50 years on, the world may require something different of this instrument. Today, states rarely threaten war against their neighbours, but many of them wreak havoc on their own peoples. International politics today is often more a matter of ethnic rather than national disagreement, of threats from terrorists rather than states. Problems that threaten stability now arise as often within as between states. Pollution can be as lethal as weapons, and spread its threats as far. You do not have to agree with all of these propositions to agree that times are changing and may require changed international systems.

In 1995 the Commission on Global Governance made proposals to address some of these issues. It envisaged ways of carrying international responsibility inside national frontiers and into matters that once were domestic responsibilities; and of making the United Nations accessible to non-state groups and even to individuals. It stressed that it was not talking about world government but about the creation of a system of global governance.[5] All these are concepts that invite ridicule or resentment in a Britain still wedded to practical and national ways of doing business. But the global issues to which they are a response are as real today as the European issues which, 40 years ago, started western Europe down the road that led to integration. They are problems which require serious attention. So do organisational proposals for tackling them.

⤳

So the OECD coalition represents effective power, the United Nations universality and legitimacy. Our third organising instrument, the Commonwealth, lacks direct power. It is global without being universal, consists of an informal gathering of disparates, seeks to reconcile widely differing interests and owes its existence to accidents of history. It is also an instrument which, quite as much as the United Nations or the European Union, arouses deep suspicions in Britain.

The Commonwealth grew out of a series of practical proposals by British statesmen and practical responses by countries of the empire as they moved towards independence. The wish to reflect a continuing sense of identity and interest while shifting political power from London to the main areas of British settlement led to the creation of the old Commonwealth. The desire of India and almost all the colonies for continuing links with the metropolis after independence led from 1947 onwards to the gradual emergence of the new Commonwealth. The Queen was universally recognised as its head, but republics were accommodated within it. So were countries such as Malaysia, Lesotho and Brunei which owed allegiance to other monarchs. And most recently the Commonwealth has begun to find a place for countries such as Mozambique which never formed part of Britain's colonial empire. In one light, the story is a triumph for practical common sense.

Seen otherwise, it is the story of a process which has created an imposing structure around a vacuum. Biennially, Commonwealth heads of government come together for discussions which quarter the globe. Some reserve for the occasion announcements of new initiatives, usually of secondary importance. In the corridors they strike useful bilateral bargains. A communiqué encapsulates the collective view of the Commonwealth on world affairs, a view which – given the variety of interests represented around the conference table – reflects a rather low Highest Common Factor of agreement. The leaders learn to understand one another better and enjoy their audiences of the Queen. But they are hard put to it to conceal the hollowness of the affair.[6]

Before we examine how the association might be given more substance, we need to establish how this came about. Even in the first half of this century the empire from which the Commonwealth sprang was anything but hollow. Soldiers from all over the empire fought in France, Flanders and on other fronts in the First World War. Between the wars trade with the empire accounted for 30 per cent of Britain's exports and imports. In India the pomp of king-emperor and viceroy reflected a great nation which was able to create in the Second World War the largest volunteer army in history, putting 2.5 million men in the field.

Each of these instances reflects a common interest – or, for the sceptical, an imposition on the colonised by the coloniser. The postwar Labour government tried to sustain it, committing itself to substantial, if belated, investment in the tropical empire. The idea of privileged trade relationships between territories in which security and order were guaranteed by imperial authority persisted into the 1950s. But gradually the things which had given the empire and the early Commonwealth substance fell away. Imperial India had been the Asian bastion of British power; republican India was specifically non-aligned, cultivating close relationships with the Soviet Union. Imperial preference surrendered before the GATT. The sterling area wilted before the dollar. Colonies emerging into independence looked for manufactured goods more attractive than Britain in the 1960s could supply. Intra-Commonwealth trade was in decline long before Britain's belated realignment with the European Economic Community. In each case, empiricism and common sense dictated choices which cumulatively diminished the trade which gave economic substance to the Commonwealth.

At the same time the Commonwealth's political contribution to stability and order was diminishing too. But it too was a reality of importance in the early postwar years. For the British four things came together: the obligations of responsible decolonisation, the Cold War rivalry for influence with the Communist powers, the need to stand up to regional tyrants, and the overarching whole which the Commonwealth idea represented. These were the considerations that kept British forces east of Suez when economic retrenchment would have called them home. They led to campaigns against insurgents in Malaya, Kenya and Cyprus, to the defence of Malaysia against outside subversion, and to expeditions to rescue from trouble more than one African Commonwealth government. But as the need or the readiness for such interventions diminished, more substance was drained from the Commonwealth association.

Throughout the years of decolonisation there were natural disagreements within the Commonwealth. It was divided for years by Britain's failure to bring the illegal regime in Rhodesia to book. Finally, Rhodesia became Zimbabwe in 1979, but after that disagreement over sanctions against apartheid South Africa set Britain at odds with the rest of the Commonwealth, and no amount of effort to isolate the issue from other, more fruitful subjects for Commonwealth discussion could stop the poison of mutual resentment spreading. To the African countries Britain appeared not just self-interested but racist. To the British, Commonwealth criticism seemed opportunistic and hypocritical. The Commonwealth "Club" endured, but as its critics within grew more vocal its defenders in turn waxed unconvincingly triumphalist.

As an operational entity therefore the Commonwealth today is diminished by contrast with the years of high hopes that followed India's emergence as a sovereign state in 1947.[7] Yet it remains a symbol of a many-sided emotional commitment, in the ceremonial Commonwealth around the Queen, and in the Commonwealth of peoples and of non-governmental groupings.[8] Few talk of leaving the Commonwealth, candidates still seek membership and France strives to build a Francophonie to emulate it. It offers privileged relationships as between friends, an informality and intimacy which the United Nations does not offer, a sounding board and a listening post, and a membership that accounts for 1.5 billion people and nearly one-third of the world's states. Its well-wishers ask themselves, as this book does, whether more could not be made of it if only a key could be found to set its operational potential free.[9]

Two particular avenues deserve exploration. The first sees the Commonwealth as a benchmark, an association which, in setting standards for itself, simultaneously sets standards for the rest of the world. Whatever the actual shortcomings of the Commonwealth's individual members, each has committed itself in principle to maintaining respectable standards of democratic politics, accountable government, transparent administration and respect for human rights. This commitment was encapsulated in the Singapore Declaration of Commonwealth Principles in 1971 and reinforced in the Harare Commonwealth Declaration 20 years later. New applicants for membership are explicitly judged by their willingness to maintain the standards of the Harare Declaration.

To the sceptic, looking at the political and human rights record of a Commonwealth member such as Kenya, this is the purest hypocrisy. To the empiricist it represents a commitment of principle on which practical advances can be based. Certainly much of the Commonwealth's work is devoted to helping members fulfil their commitments under the Singapore and Harare Declarations. It monitors elections in Commonwealth countries, unites Commonwealth lawyers in discussion of the common law, trains Commonwealth tax administrators, customs officers and policemen. Research and colloquia provide intellectual underpinning.[10] The Commonwealth Fund for Technical Co-operation provides mutual expertise. The work is worthy, painstaking, unspectacular. Over the decades it can raise standards but it is not the kind of programme to set the pulse racing. And the Commonwealth's practical work always depends on the political will of its members; each time a country like Nigeria throws its undertakings out of the window, the ambition to see the Commonwealth as a true benchmark recedes further into the distance.

For Britain the concept nevertheless provides a focus for much of its work in the developing world. More than half of British bilateral development assistance goes to Commonwealth countries. Many of them are important British markets. Order, good government, transparency, free markets make the pursuit of British interests easier and safer. If Commonwealth countries gradually achieve higher standards in all these fields they will bring credit not just to themselves but to the country which remains the association's most influential member. The success of the Commonwealth as a benchmark of behaviour for others as well as its own members is a British priority, one worth the modest investment of the resources, effort, hopes and frequent disappointments it requires.

The second way to give greater operational substance to the Commonwealth may be more fanciful but could take it to higher ground. It is the concept of the Commonwealth as an organising instrument, a global if not universal organisation to stand at the United Nations' right hand.

The Charter of the United Nations envisages a major problem solving role for regional organisations. For example, the European Union played its part in Bosnia and the Organisation of African Unity in Rwanda. The Commonwealth is in a sense a regional organisation, with the difference that its members happen to be bound together by historical inheritance rather than by geography. In a world that is seeing the death of geography, physical distance is no longer an obstacle to understanding and cooperation.[11] The globe-circling Commonwealth has useful operational assets. Its members have a working language in common, a shared legal and administrative inheritance and a style of informal cooperation beside which United Nations procedures are formalistic and politicised. The Commonwealth undertakes international tasks such as the attempt to cajole Nigeria back to democracy which might otherwise land directly on the United Nations' table.

Britain has an interest in furthering the development of the Commonwealth as an organising instrument. Already it provides a grouping of value to its members, particularly the smaller ones whose voice it magnifies. It can help resolve problems for them and between them. It can undertake tasks on behalf of the United Nations, often more effectively and economically. As its only permanent Security Council member, Britain can critically influence its interplay with the United Nations. The process can bring some relief to the United Nations and some benefit to the world. And a Commonwealth with a real role will be healthier in itself and in its relationship with outsiders.

There are some who want Britain to aim higher and reinstate the Commonwealth as a concern of British policy comparable with the European Union and the Atlantic Alliance. In 1996 the Foreign Affairs Committee of the House of Commons argued for such a higher profile.[12] It noted the good will towards the Commonwealth which it encountered on its overseas missions, and criticised the British government's neglect of the organisation, in particular of the potential of its member countries in south-east Asia and the Pacific Rim. It believed that Britain should consciously build on its Commonwealth connections so as to increase its room for manoeuvre in the world outside Europe and the North Atlantic. But it faltered when it came to identifying major themes and opportunities for this more salient policy.

When the Labour government came to office in 1997 it similarly placed greater emphasis on the Commonwealth. It immediately published a new mission statement for the Foreign and Commonwealth Office which stated as one of its principal strategic aims: "to strengthen the Commonwealth and to improve the prosperity of its members and co-operation between its members". It did not document ways of achieving it and the Commonwealth heads of government meeting in Edinburgh in October 1997 made no greater impact than earlier ones in the biennial series, demonstrating once again the difficulty of giving real operational purpose to a disparate organisation. I have encountered the same difficulty. I value what the Commonwealth does already but can identify no strategic ways of doing more with and through the organisation than a painstaking pursuit of the Commonwealth as a benchmark and the development on a case-by-case basis of the Commonwealth as an organising instrument.[13]

There may be a fourth possible contributor to global order. Its elements look tenuous beside the OECD coalition, the United Nations and the Commonwealth. It is not an organisation and has no formal structure. Yet a range of factors already in play in the world's game may, taken together, constitute a new force for world order, a sort of civil society to put beside the world of governments and official organisations. Commercial interests that already ignore frontiers, the non-governmental bodies which circle the globe, private charity on an international scale and the millions of individuals who now know the world, and hence know one another, all these bind the world together. Each of them has a vested interest in peace, stability and cooperation. The new information and communication technologies make it easier for them to work together. They have a potential as great as that of the formal organisations. The question is whether they can mobilise it.

Firstly, international business. Its investment far outweighs official development assistance. In the developing world and in the countries in transition from Communism it sets new standards of effectiveness. Within a generation it can transform conditions of life for millions in the developing countries in which it settles, as places like Thailand and Malaysia testify. Within another generation its beneficiaries begin to demand a political voice to go with their new economic status. In the long run international business is likely to see its interests better served by governments which accommodate them rather than repress them. No more than national governments is international business beyond reproach; but in the developing world it does more good than harm; and part of that good is a contribution to freedom and well-being, and hence to order.

Non-governmental bodies make perhaps as great a contribution. They constantly interact with the United Nations system.[14] They are as numerous as the actors in international business, and though they lack the financial muscle at the disposal of the business sector, they have as much political influence. A few, such as the Red Cross, have roots which go back to the 19th century. Others date from the first half of the 20th. But it is the years since the Second World War that have seen their full development. Their growth runs parallel with the global spread of self-government, with the explosion of knowledge about distant places and with the acceptance of the truth that humanity is truly inseparable. Such non-governmental bodies contribute in two ways to the development of global order: through the influence they can bring to bear on national governments and official international organisations; and through the effects of the work they themselves undertake. Like international business, they walk difficult tight-ropes, not always successfully. But in places like Rwanda they help alleviate the tragedies which make a mockery of expressions like "global order".

International charity is the business of many non-governmental bodies, but it needs to be considered separately. It focuses on those who are as vulnerable in a united world as they used to be in a divided one. Its essential work is the transfer of resources from rich to poor, requited only in moral, ethical and sometimes spiritual terms. It has the potential to make a major contribution to world order, by alleviating the poverty and distress which threaten order and by expressing the belief that we are all our brother's keeper. Private international charity is a purer expression of global solidarity than official development assistance and international business.

Brought together by a growing awareness of their own importance and their own need for a stable world system in which to operate, these forces already have as much impact on the nature of international society as the governmental and inter-governmental organisations with which most of this chapter has been concerned. Their political and social influence is more implicit than explicit, but nevertheless profound. They have contacts and interconnections which rival those of the official world. The advances of information and communication technologies enhance their effectiveness and show the world their significance. The growth in their importance in the world community parallels changes within national societies. Britain's business world, its non-governmental organisations and its charities are more agile and articulate than most; in their international activities they can make a contribution to international stability and order that is greater than most. In doing so they serve their country as well as the world community.

1   Francis Fukuyama, *The End of History and the Last Man* (London: Hamish Hamilton, 1992).

2   Rosemary Righter, *Utopia Lost. The United Nations and World Order* (New York: Twentieth Century Fund, 1995).

3   Brian Urquhart, *A Life in Peace and War* (London: Weidenfeld & Nicolson, 1987).

4   Evan Luard, *The United Nations: How it Works and What it Does* (2nd edn. London, 1994).

5   *Our Global Neighbourhood, The Report of the Commission on Global Governance* (Oxford: Oxford University Press, 1995).

6   See *The Commonwealth at the Summit,* Vols 1 and 2, (London: Commonwealth Secretariat, 1987 and 1997 respectively).

7   It is remarkable, for example, that there is no reference to the Commonwealth, a global grouping of nations which embraces many different civilisations, in the index to Samuel P Huntington's book, *The Clash of Civilizations and the Remaking of World Order* (New York: Simon & Schuster, 1996).

8   For an impression of the range of Commonwealth cooperation see *Directory of Commonwealth Organisations* (London: Commonwealth Secretariat, 1991).

9   Denis Judd, *Empire: The British Imperial Experience from 1765 to the Present* (London: HarperCollins, 1996).

10 See, for example, *International Economic Issues. Contributions by the Commonwealth 1975–1990* (London: Commonwealth Secretariat, 1990).

11 Frances Cairncross, *The Death of Distance* (London: Orion, 1997).

12 *The Future Role of the Commonwealth. Foreign Affairs Committee First Report* (London: HMSO, 1996).

13 Rob Jenkins, *Reassessing the Commonwealth* (London: Royal Institute of International Affairs, 1997).

14 Peter Willetts (ed.), *The Conscience of the World* (London: Hurst, 1996).

14　The right choices for Britain

The time has come to summarise where Britain belongs in the world. It is best done in terms of choices.

The first choice is between heart and head, emotion and calculation. Here the traditional foreign policy practitioner sees no contest, for he is convinced that head and calculation must prevail. But we have seen that Britain's heart has often had as much influence as calculation in shaping its view of the world. Emotion warms popular feeling towards the United States as it chills attitudes towards Japan. It has been as prominent as reason in the arguments about Britain's relationships with the European Union and its continental neighbours. It helps shape attitudes towards a continuing world role for Britain and its commitment to world order. When world affairs arouse attention in Britain, emotion rather than intellect better captures the mood of the moment and the will of the people. By the same token, the worst failure of Britain's elite and foreign policy establishment has been their inability to carry the man in the street along with their foreign policies.

Many factors today give emotion an enhanced say in foreign as in other policies. Deference to the opinion of the expert is declining. Political antennae are more sharply tuned to the popular will. The descent of the largely foreign-owned print media into ever cruder simplification feeds an emotional rather than a considered expression of what the people want. Televised politics is dominated by the sound-bite, which appeals to instinct rather than complicated reasoning. So the answer to our first choice must be "both". Policy must respect the emotions of the British people and politicians must formulate it in terms which make sense to their hearts as well as their heads. And yet, in a world where there is less margin for error than there has been in the past, our political leaders and our public servants must ensure that the essence of policy is intellectually rigorous, deals in hard and often unpalatable realities, and serves clearly formulated long-term British interests. The old-fashioned qualities of empathy and leadership are needed to bridge the gap between calculation and emotion, respecting the importance of both.

The second choice the British face is between involvement in and aloofness from the doings of the rest of the world. Delight in standing alone has a long pedigree, from Shakespeare's sceptred isle to Churchill's growled defiance, "If necessary, alone". But so, equally, has British involvement in the affairs of others. When Shakespeare wrote, Drake was singeing the King of Spain's beard. When Churchill spoke, Britain's ally France had been driven out of the war and a British army had just made its escape from the continent. And since Shakespeare's time and Churchill's, the balance has tilted ever further towards involvement in affairs beyond our shores. The sea is no longer a reliable moat, abroad has become part of our everyday lives, we need foreign goods and services and investment, and the very idea of inviolate nationhood has given way to something more complex and modulated. Isolation now is the purest romanticism, unattainable and undesirable.

The third choice is between involvement in the world on our own or in cooperation with others, and here too both options have a respectable pedigree. Britain fought the revolutionary and Napoleonic wars in coalition with continental allies, but it ruled the waves for most of the 19th century in arrogant isolation. Then, in 1904, it entered into the entente cordiale with France, and its history ever since has been one of commitment – if often disappointed and embittered commitment – to one ally, alliance and partnership after another. Faith in the Atlantic Alliance and the European Community has long represented orthodoxy in British foreign-policy making, and arguments for going it alone instead have come increasingly to look like perversity.[1] Instance after instance in earlier chapters points to the desirability, even the inevitability, for Britain of doing business in cooperation and partnership with others. The country is weaker than it was. The affairs of the world are more complex. International and domestic considerations are intertwined. A state resolute to go it alone would cut itself off from an immense variety of international intercourse. North Korea and Cuba are illustrations of the price that has to be paid for elected or enforced isolation, just as Switzerland illustrates the pros and cons of a very different kind of self-sufficiency. For a Britain that ceased to bestride the world like a colossus a century ago, partners and associates are essential.

Its most obvious partners are to be found in Europe and North America, and the next choice is to which should we give priority. Most Britons instinctively turn first to the United States, and if they were asked for reasons they would point to history, language, importance and reliability. Other instincts turn instead to Europe. Reason recognises the importance to Britain of both and rejects a stark choice between them. But we still have to decide on which leg, the Atlantic or the continental, we want to put most of our weight. If you accept the arguments of earlier chapters, the conclusion is clear. Britain is both an Atlantic and a European power. It needs the Atlantic Alliance as well as the European Union. It needs the United States more than it needs any one of its European partners. But its major European partners are about its equal: the United States mightier by far. Their interests and vulnerabilities are similar to Britain's: the United States' increasingly divergent from it. If we had to choose we should choose Europe, not the United States, and work to make the European Union a superpower in its own right. But we do not need to make that choice, for the Atlantic and European relationships are not antithetical but complementary. A satisfactory Atlantic relationship demands a Europe that speaks and acts in approximate harmony. For Britain, Brussels is not an alternative to Washington; but concord in Brussels is an essential prerequisite to effectiveness in Washington. So the answer to the question to whom we should turn between the United States and Europe is "Both – but Europe first".

It is tempting to ask what kind of Europe the British want, and to classify the reply in terms of choice between alliance of independent states, confederation or federation. But in the real world there is no such choice. The European Union already embodies some characteristics of each. All the Union's members have committed themselves to the pursuit of "an ever closer union of the peoples of Europe" in that gloriously ambiguous phrase of the Treaty of Rome. Its draftsmen did not define the phrase, nor how fast or how far the process would go; but the commitment binds all member states and the process is one which most of them are happy to pursue. For Britain to advocate some alternative process would achieve nothing beyond reawakening doubts about our commitment to a European Union in which most Britons believe. So the right course for Britain is as whole-hearted a commitment to "ever closer union" as it can bring itself to embrace. The process is likely to lead in time to a European Union much more closely integrated than it is today, perhaps a recognisable federation, perhaps even a United States of Europe. Britain will be better off contributing to its development than proposing fanciful alternatives, as a committed insider rather than a whimsical spectator.

There are economic choices to be fought over within the European Union. On the one side stands the economic libertarianism of the free market, on the other the paternalism of the social market economy. There are elements of both in the national economies of each of the Union's members, but at the moment Britain stands at one end of the continuum, France at the other. The choice will be played out in national policy-making and in the slow unwinding of one argument after another in Brussels. It will affect the internal nature of the European Union and the face it turns to the global economy. The British people seem to want the best of both worlds, the individual benefits that the free market brings them, together with the social protection and security that its rival claims to provide. Whether Europe can in fact combine the two will be a test of its long-term economic capacity to compete with North America and Asia and of its political maturity.

Do we want an open Europe or a closed one ? The need to develop the European Union in parallel with a continuing commitment to the Atlantic relationship provides part of the answer. So does the need to play a full competitive part in the global economy. But other considerations are more ambivalent. What sort of face should Europe turn, for example, to migrants, to the Moslem world and to the poor of the earth? For Britain, more involved with the world outside Europe than any of its European partners, the basic choice is simple. Our overseas interests and obligations should make us want not Fortress Europe but a Europe which forms part of a global economy and which accepts its responsibilities in one world.

What should we make of proposals that Britain should attach itself more closely than its European partners to individual countries, regions or groupings: to the United States, for example, or to the Old Commonwealth, the Commonwealth as a whole, Japan, or east Asia? As we have seen, they are more seductive in theory than they would be in the implementation. None of them provides a satisfactory alternative to a commitment to an open, outward-looking Europe. But in a supporting rather than a principal role they have considerable merits. In the United States we should make what use we can of historical links and common language, of the interpenetration of British and American business and intellectual worlds, of a long and continuing experience of the two governments working together at every level, and of our own unique ability to talk policy and global issues with American policy-makers on equal terms. In Asia we have historical links and some present reputation. In the Commonwealth we have both cousins in North America and the Antipodes and privileged access to an extraordinary cross-section of the world's peoples. We must beware of grab-bag globalism, but we must take all the opportunities history has bequeathed us, to supplement a strategy centred on Europe and the Atlantic. It will be easier to seize them as a leading and active member of the European Union, and therefore as a more attractive partner for political, economic and business decision-makers in other continents.

The globe is full of challenges that we can see as threats or opportunities. The world of Islam is one, the disorder left by the collapse of Communism another. So is the need for cooperation to face new threats, such as environmental pollution, international crime, political terrorism, single-issue obsession and world poverty. Here too, Britain has a choice, between whole-hearted engagement and the enjoyment of its own relatively favoured position. There are arguments for the latter, not least the sheer intractability of the problems which the former course would have to tackle. But these are truly global problems; no part of the earth can hope to escape their consequences. Specific British interests are threatened by each of these problems, from a hijacked British Airways flight to babies threatened by skin cancer on British beaches. So self-interest argues for engagement. So does altruism: for the sake of those we help today and of our own consciences tomorrow.

The last choice concerns British commitment to global order: to the

United Nations, the Commonwealth, peace-keeping, international standards of government and human rights. Here again Britain has a strong position, too strong in the eyes of those who see us as the victims still of the temptations of global overstretch. We were central to the creation of the United Nations and the emergence of the modern Commonwealth. We have our Security Council seat, a Commonwealth centred on London and the attention of a lot of people who value our international contribution. We have armed forces well-suited to peace-keeping, peace-making and the amelioration of human and natural disaster, as well as the official and non-governmental organisations that can back them up. But why should we commit these resources? Once again, self-interest is one answer. Need is a second. Altruism could be a third.

Those are the choices we face and those are the answers I believe make most sense for Britain. They bring us back to three convictions that pervade this book. First, Britain has declined but it has not failed : it is an effective and important player in the world's game. Second, the problems of the new world which have emerged since 1989 demand just as wholehearted a commitment to working with others as did our wartime alliances, or NATO, or all the other cooperative ventures to which we are bound. Third, Britain must commit itself wholeheartedly to Europe, the European Union and the European adventure. To do so will bring us benefits inside Europe and out: we will be able to help shape Europe to our liking, and we can use the European Union's clout to promote European and British interests in the wider world.

Through these commitments – to faith in ourselves, to partnerships with others and to the Europe in which we belong – we will find emotional, intellectual and material contentment and so satisfy the demands of our hearts, of our minds and of our interests alike.

1   See for example three attempts by the Royal Institute of International Affairs to encapsulate British foreign policy: Kenneth Younger, *Changing Perspectives in British Foreign Policy* (1964), Christopher Tugendhat and William Wallace, *Options for British Foreign Policy in the 1990s* (1988) and Laurence Martin, *British Foreign Policy, Challenges and Choices for the 21st Century* (1997).